POETRY DIMENSION
ANNUAL 5

Edited by DANNIE ABSE

POETRY DIMENSION

ANNUAL 5

The Best of The Poetry Year

 Robson Books

FIRST PUBLISHED IN GREAT BRITAIN IN 1978
BY ROBSON BOOKS LTD., 28 POLAND STREET,
LONDON W1V 3DB. THIS COLLECTION COPYRIGHT
©DANNIE ABSE 1978

Acknowledgements are owed to the authors whose work has been reprinted here and which remains their copyright: also to those publishers and periodicals named below the prose and poems printed in these pages. The Publishers acknowledge with thanks the assistance of the Arts Council and the editor wishes to express his gratitude to Mr. Jonathan Barker of the Arts Council Poetry Library.

The full text of 'The Critic as Vandal' is published by The Oxford University Press under the title *Wording and Re-Wording: Paraphrases in Literary Criticism*. Martin Dodsworth's 'On Donald Davie' was first commissioned for an Open University course on 20th Century Poetry, and the Open University's permission to reprint it here is gratefully acknowledged.

Addresses of the small publishers whose publications have provided poems for this year's annual include:

The Aquila Publishing Co. Ltd: P.O. Box 1, Portree, Isle of Skye. *Blackstaff Press Ltd:* 255A Upper New Townards Road, Belfast. *Carcanet Press Ltd:* 266 Councillor Lane, Cheadle Hulme, Cheadle, Cheshire. *Harry Chambers/Peterloo Poets:* 8 Cavendish Road, Heaton Mersey, Stockport. *London Magazine Editions:* 30 Thurloe Place, London S.W.7. *The Mandeville Press:* 2 Taylor's Hill, Hitchin, Hertfordshire. *The Menard Press:* 23 Fitzwarren Gardens, London N.19. *Rondo Publications:* 123 The Albany, Old Hall Street, Liverpool.

Poetry dimension annual.
5.
1. English poetry — 20th century
I. Abse, Dannie
831'.9'1408   PR1225

ISBN 0-86051-012-3
ISBN 0-86051-013-1   Pbk

Printed photolitho in England by
Ebenezer Baylis & Son Ltd
The Trinity Press, Worcester, and London

CONTENTS

Poems from Magazines

Lives of the Poets

Introductory Note

Four years or so ago, Anthony Thwaite discussed in *The Two Poetries** the common reader's response to verse being written now in Britain. He remarked, with sad resignation, on the popularity of that oral poetry cradled in Liverpool, and more importantly, he drew attention to the revulsion of many University graduates towards verse that had academic sanction simply because of its complexity. This revulsion stemmed, he suggested, from the aridities of their Eng. Lit. education. 'They (the students) had been through the mill, Thwaite wrote, 'and had come out as chaff. Years of *Tradition and the Individual Talent, Principles of Literary Criticism, Seven Types of Ambiguity*, and *Revaluation* (with all the derivatives and by-products of these) had made them incapable of looking at literature with other than an over-subtlety, an ingenuity, as fatigued as it was detachable. *Criticism* stank in their nostrils.'

Recently, Philip Larkin, in an address in Hamburg on accepting the 1976 Shakespeare Prize (the last poet to receive this prize was John Masefield in 1938!) returned to similar themes: the inadequacies of both the mindless simplicities of oral poetry and the academically structured poems built out of fragmented artifacts of literature rather than life. But instead of focusing on the reader's response to such poems Philip Larkin was concerned with the poets themselves who might be tempted unconsciously, because of material reward, to write in a certain way so that they might star on the Poetry Circuit or advance on the Campus:

* Reprinted in *Poetry Dimension Annual 2*

7

In the Seventies it has become possible . . . to make a living, if not by poetry, then at least by being a poet. Take poetry readings, for example: what Dylan Thomas called 'travelling 200 miles just to recite, in my fruity voice, poems that would not be appreciated and could, anyway, be read in books.' If by such readings a poet enables his audience to understand his poems more fully, and so to enjoy them more, this is good. But if doing so tempts him to begin writing the kind of poems that succeed only in front of an audience, he may start to deal in instant emotion, instant opinion, instant sound and fury, and this may not be so good...

The same kind of danger awaits the poet on the campus. If literature is a good thing, then exegesis and analysis can only demonstrate its goodness, and lead to fresh and deeper ways of enjoying it. But if the poet engages in this exegesis and analysis by becoming a university teacher, the danger is that he will begin to assume unconsciously that the more a poem can be analysed – and therefore the more it needs to be analysed – the better poem it is, and he may in consequence, again unconsciously, start to write the kind of poem that is earning him a living . . .

All this may be obvious but it needs saying loud and often. Fortunately those writers who produce oral pieces for the microphone do not pose any durable threat. They may bamboozle an untutored audience for a while, and this, of course, is to be regretted. But once their poems are visible on the page so too are their limitations. Rather it is the poem that has been wilfully or unconsciously structured so that it may be disentangled by a critic short on feeling but high on invention that is the more pernicious danger. If such critics, despite their erudition, were less naive there would be fewer poems that consisted only of ambiguity and footnote.

Certainly no poems of this kind are to be found in this annual nor, indeed, any of the platform variety. They have all been taken from magazines

8

and books* published in Britain between March 1976 and March 1977. Despite the usual shortage of interesting criticism, and instant poems and cross-word puzzle academic verse notwithstanding, it seems to me to have been a good year.

D.A.

<hr/>

* All the books are by British poets. There was not space to include any of the many translations that appeared or poems by those American poets – Daniel Hoffman, Louis Simpson, James Merrill, Anne Sexton, Richard Eberhart, etc. – who had books published in the U.K. during this time period.

Points of View

I want to make this essay an exercise in ground-clearing. There cannot ever have been a subject about which so many contradictory opinions are expressed as this of the social involvement of imaginative art; and, though my brief is about poetry, most of the conclusions I have come to could be equally well applied to painting, or the theatre or prose fiction (even, with some adjustments, to music, in so far as music gets dragged into this kind of *imbroglio* at all). The area within which I would like to tidy up can be indicated by these questions:

Is there anything in the nature of a moral obligation on the poet to convey opinions *in his work* about the sickness or health of the society he finds himself living in?

In the major poetry of our tradition, has social criticism been a preponderant theme or has it taken its place as one theme among many?

In responding to poetry which overtly sets out to make social judgments, ought we to apply any specialised criteria, or do we just approach it as poetry like any other?

And, most flatly of all; can poetry ever be straight propaganda? or, if you prefer — can straight propaganda ever be poetry?

All of us who write are familiar with the person who comes up to us, on an average about once every three weeks in some shape and size, and asks, "Why don't you use your writing to strive for a better world?" His (or her) tone will suggest, with a flavour of accusation, that the writer is heartlessly frivolous, or perhaps cynical, to leave so obvious a duty undone. A writer, with the power to attract people's attention, to engage their feelings, to channel their emotions in this and that direction — surely a writer, of all people, ought to put on shining armour and slay the dragon. The dragon, of course, always turns out to be the easily identified villain of whatever mythology the questioner has embraced. Capitalism, imperialism, racism, fascism, discrimination of all kinds — there is no shortage of dragons, wearing conspicuous labels. And if one hesitates to dismantle one's art and rebuild it as a missile-launcher, the hesitation does not necessarily stem from any complacency about the world as it is. Personally I am just as convinced as anyone that human society ought to be changed; its cruelty and cynicism appal me; its greed and competitiveness and prodigality leave me saddened; its ugliness affronts me. And the misbehaviour of mankind is all the more horrible in that it takes place on such a beautiful planet as the earth. We are like a lot of delinquent children who break into a handsome house, full of fine furniture assembled with love and good taste, and proceed to relieve ourselves all over it. Yes, I agree that the world should be changed! But are the imaginative arts the most suitable instrument for bringing this change about? If you use a razor to chop wood, don't you end up with very little wood and a spoilt razor, no longer any use for its real purpose?

I am quite aware that the dedicated political activist will answer at once, *so much the worse for art.* To such minds, nothing matters except the struggle to change the world: indeed, to let anything else matter, to give attention to personal relationships or undirected art or the beauty of nature or abstract intellectual questions, is merely immoral. It is easy to feel small in the presence of such single-mindedness. On the other hand, the single vision is usually a tunnel vision: it achieves its clarity at the cost of a Draconian exclusiveness. To see a single set of issues with such intense clarity is usually a sign that there are other issues one is wilfully not seeing. And here comes the fundamental split. The narrow, fiercely directed vision of the revolutionary, or for that matter of the mystic or the martyr, is entirely different from, entirely irreconcilable with, the temperament that produces art. (*So much the worse for art!* again.) But so much the better for it too, in view of the rich and contradictory nature of human experience. "Why don't you face facts?" someone asked E. M. Forster. "How can I", he replied "when they're all round me?"

Louis MacNeice, in his book on Yeats, had some wise words to say about poetry and propaganda, writing at a time when the claims of propaganda were being pressed as they are today.

> The propaganda poets claim to be realists — a claim which can only be correct if realism is identical with pragmatism. Truth, whether poetic or scientific, tends as often as not to be neither simple nor easily intelligible, whereas the propagandist is bound by his function to give his particular public something that they can easily swallow and digest. Realism, in the proper sense of the word, takes account of facts regardless of their propaganda value and records not only those facts which suit one particular public

but also those facts which suit another public and even those facts which suit no one. The propagandist may have his "truth" but it is not the truth of the scientist or of the realist; it is even further removed from these than poetic truth is. He is only interested in changing the world; any use of words therefore which will lead to that end — lies, distortions, or outrageous over-simplifications — will, from his point of view, be true. This again is a tenable position but it does not prove either that the poet will write better poetry by substituting propagandist truth for poetic truth or even that it is the poet's duty as a man to write propaganda poetry. Even if the poet believes in the *end* of the propagandist he can have legitimate doubts whether that end will be in the long run usefully served by a prostitution of poetry. Poetry is to some extent, like mathematics, an autotelic activity; if bad poetry or bad mathematics is going to further a good cause, let us leave this useful abuse of these arts to people who are not mathematicians or poets.

So coolly and so cogently argued, the case would be seen to carry itself. But there are very powerful magnets pulling in the other direction. A good many writers, like a good many people of every kind, have found themselves, at some stage in their lives, participating in some activist movement or other. The hankering for corporate action, for shared ideals, shared burdens, shared discipline and danger, comes over most people at times. In the particular case of the writer, there are some causes that make him particularly vulnerable.

In the first place, a writer's life is lonely. If he gets on with his work without the nuisance of other people, he is also deprived of their comfort and support. After a number of years in the trade, most people manage to come to terms with this loneliness, but it is particularly hard to bear for young writers, who are in consequence always forming groups, and issuing manifestos, and gathering in excited bunches. Often, this impulse takes a political turn, and then the young writer has the delicious heady sensation of being wanted. "We need you. Our point of view should be stated by someone like you with a gift for words."

This kind of invitation is music in a young writer's ears, and virtually the only way for him to hear it is to join a group who are pushing towards some pre-defined objective. Otherwise, however well he writes, nobody will claim him, and young writers want to be claimed. Such group solidarity will, necessarily, lead him often into solemn fatuity.

All my life I seem to have been opening magazines and books on poetry and finding solemn fatuities based on political attitudes. In the 1940s, I promise you, someone actually perpetrated the couplet:

> *Bare, bitter with the truth, not posed, not slick,*
> *Here's verse that's more than good, it's Bolshevik.*

But the risk of fatuity is, to some, easier to take than the certainty of loneliness. The subject-matter of art is, necessarily, as generalised as the scope of human experience itself. Poetry is about life, death, love, hate, heaven, hell, immortality, joy and pain. But these things are everybody's concern: and what is everybody's concern can often seem like nobody's concern. Whereas if he writes a poem arguing fiercely that the Palestinian people must have their rights, or Basque militants be let out of prison, or the British Army must get out of/stay in Northern Ireland, he will find himself addressing a large, ready-made sector of the public who are looking for someone to say just *that*. And he will be welcomed, and fêted. It is all an illusion, of course. The welcome will turn to suspicion, the cordiality to venom, as soon as he deserts the narrow path of that particular subject-matter and goes back to his real work of writing about unfenced-in human experience. Then he will find out what it is like to try to get down from a tiger's back. But till that moment comes, the ride can be very exhilarating.

Then again there is the grudging tribute of envy that practical, demonstrable action always receives from those bound to the desk or the easel. I always sympathise with the writer, whoever it was (it was Augustus Birrell who told the story), who attended a court sitting, and at the end of the morning's business remarked ruefully, "When that judge sentences some poor devil to go to prison for five years, he goes. But when I publish a book, nothing happens!" In view of the sheer number of things that have happened because books were published, this attitude seems to me unrealistic. Anything that involves people's thoughts and feelings must surely accomplish more in the way of results than the pronouncements of a bewigged and ermined figure who is merely implementing the law that has been established as much by the writing of books as by anything else. But the attitude, understandably, persists, as witness Auden's lines in the elegy on Yeats.

> *For poetry makes nothing happen: it survives*
> *In the valley of its saying where executives*
> *Would never want to tamper; it flows south*
> *From ranches of isolation and busy griefs,*
> *Raw towns that we believe and die in; it survives,*
> *A way of happening, a mouth.*

I find those lines memorable and somehow comforting, but they contain a number of statements that seem to me untrue: To begin with, executives (party bosses, for instance) very definitely claim the right to "tamper" with poetry if it seems likely to talk back to them; and by that tampering they tacitly admit that "the valley of its saying" is a valley along which important rivers may flow — perhaps that same "peasant river" that was "untempted by the fashionable quays" earlier on in the same poem. And if poetry, and all art, survives mainly as "a mouth", a mouth is useful not only for making noises but for receiving nourishment.

Still, the point is that the writer, particularly the young writer, doesn't *feel* as if anything happened when he publishes his thoughts; they don't seem anything like actions. Hence the almost irresistible pull of activism to the literary temperament, the kind of thing we read about in Renee Winegarten's fascinating *Writers and Revolution,* aptly subtitled "The fatal lure of action". One of Mrs Winegarten's prize exhibits is Baudelaire. His view of the human condition, that its ills were totally incurable, that the human animal was only at home in a jungle full of cruelty and ferocity, and that the beauty of life was to be found in the strange and lurid flowers that grew out of this evil, and nowhere else — this view would surely inoculate anyone against the temptation to participate in schemes for the radical change of society. Yet Baudelaire was seen by friends, during the rising of 1848, among a crowd that had just looted a gunsmith's shop, waving a gun and shouting slogans with the best of them.

I am equally fascinated by some examples that do not find their way into Mrs Winegarten's muster. When the Spanish people rose against Ferdinand VII and the Inquisition, well-wishers in England raised a sum of money to help them, and two young Cambridge men carried this money to a secret rendezvous in the Pyrenees, to hand it over to the rebel leaders. The two young Cambridge men were Alfred Tennyson and Arthur Hallam. The future author of *Idylls of the King* and the *Ode on the Death of the Duke of Wellington,* accompanied by the man whose death was to inspire *In Memoriam,* bringing aid and comfort to desperadoes in a mountain hide-out!

Of course it is not only writers who are tempted by the cosy togetherness of group action, and the short-term satisfaction of doing something that has a demonstrable effect. But the loneliness of a writer's life makes him, especially in youth, vulnerable to the need for power. He wants to *matter* to somebody, instead of being politely tolerated and half-heartedly encouraged because literature is a Good Thing. And it is not lost on him that the individual who is committed to a cause outside himself, who is prepared, or appears to be prepared, to stake his entire life on the chance of making his ideal come true, is a very attractive figure: that he has, to use the word that we have conspired to burgle from the theologians, *charisma.* Even if the writer did not know this from life, literature itself would instruct him that it is so. Think of Turgenev's *On the Eve*! Think of Elena, the intelligent, nervous, receptive Russian girl of good family, who has the love of the decent young man of her own class, Andrei Bersenyev, and could easily win that of the artist Shubin: but it is neither of these she wants. The man who captivates her is Dmitri Nikanorovitch Insarov, the withdrawn, austere Bulgarian exile, who takes no notice of her until she begins to share his passion for the one shining ideal of his life, the liberation of Bulgaria from Turkish rule.

To identify with a movement, to enjoy the admiration and loyalty of those who can see the beauty of a life given to the struggle for a tangible objective, must often seem to a writer the solution of his personal problems. But then, if the writer can't face personal problems, and a lot of them, he shouldn't be a writer. And having accepted the profession, or to speak more accurately the vocation, or to speak more accurately still the condition, of authorship, one of the things he needs to learn is the extent to which the social and political situation, the general experience which impinges on him neither more nor less than on thousands of others, is a material that he can work into art: the extent, and the means.

The starting and finishing point, of course, are his experiences as an individual. It will sometimes happen that a cluster of events describable as political will elicit a response from his entire being: it will affect him morally, imaginatively, emotionally, and the work he produces will unite all these.

Sometimes, when a large-scale political event erupts across the world, the reaction of poets is strange in the same way as the behaviour of the dog which attracts the notice of Sherlock Holmes.

– Is there anything else to which you wish to draw my attention?
– Only the singular incident of the dog in the night-time.
– The dog did nothing in the night-time.
– That is the singular incident.

The most extraordinary occasion in our century when the dog did nothing in the night-time, I suppose was the gradual disaffection of Western Communists in the wake of Stalin's betrayal of the Left. When the Russian people rose and threw off their Czars and their landlords, and proclaimed that power was now in the hands of the poor, young and generous people in every country in the world promptly fell in love with Russia. And when news began to leak out that the first, genuinely popular phase of the Revolution had been quickly succeeded by a cool power-grabbing operation, by a group of dedicated and ruthless conspirators, when it began to be reported that the Russian people, having formerly been whipped with whips, were now being whipped with scorpions, of course these same generous-minded young rejected such reports as the expected backlash of counter-revolutionary propaganda, the sort of thing the bourgeois enemy would be bound to say. Time went by, the generous-minded young became less young and perhaps a shade less generous-minded, but they still believed in Russia and they associated this belief with Stalin. Stalin was Russia and Russia was the Revolution, so how could he be wrong?

From this position they were dislodged, in a series of sickening jolts. Some fell off with the Nazi-Soviet pact in 1939; others with the refusal to permit free elections in the Soviet zone of Germany immediately after the War, and the subsequent bagging of an Eastern European empire; the last and biggest layer fell off after the bludgeoning of Hungary in 1956. A few, of course, never fell off. There are still hard-shell Stalinists who take the line that Stalin was right by definition, so if murder and treachery were committed by Stalin, then murder and treachery must be right. In this spirit, we must assume, did the poet Hugh McDiarmid rejoin the Communist Party in 1956, after being out of it for some years, and declare that those who left were a bunch of softies and the Party was "well shot of them".

The hard-shell survivors made their attitudes abundantly clear: but what of those who fell off? What inward struggles, torments, questionings, final resolutions, did they undergo? And why did the poets among them not bring this material into their poems? No doubt there are many poems I have missed; but I have read a great many poems written in the 1930s, '40s and '50s, many of them by Socialists, and I do not remember a single one that dealt with the agony of withdrawing one's loyalty from Stalin, formerly the all-hallowed Leader.

The situation can be seen in all its singularity if we compare it with the exactly parallel sequence of events that happened some hundred and thirty years earlier. When the French people rose and threw off their monarchy and aristocracy, and declared a revolutionary democracy, young and generous people in every country fell in love with France. And when the revolutionary society brought forth the *Grande Armée* with Napoleon at its head, there were still people in every country who felt that Napoleon must be right, because Napoleon was France and France was the Revolution.

When Napoleon was finally broken at Waterloo, the occasion was one of exultation for the bulk of the English people; at last the suffering of the Napoleonic Wars was over, at last there had been a great victory for British arms. But for "progressives", who had never been able to slough off a certain awe of Napoleon and had clung to a certain identification with France, the day was a sad one. Benjamin Robert Haydon's diary has a famous page about the effect first on himself, then by contrast on Leigh Hunt and William Hazlitt.

> ". . . I ran back again to Scott's. They were gone to bed, but I knocked them up and said, 'The Duke has beat Napoleon, taken one hundred and fifty pieces of cannon, and is marching to Paris.'

Scott began to ask questions. I said, 'None of your questions; it's a fact,' and both of us said 'Huzza!'

"I went home and to bed; got up and to work. Sammons, my model and corporal of the 2nd Life Guards, came, and we tried to do our duty; but Sammons was in such a fidget about his regiment charging, and I myself was in such a heat, I was obliged to let him go. Away he went, and I never saw him till late the next day, and then he came drunk with talking. I read the *Gazette* the last thing before going to bed. I dreamt of it and was fighting all night; I got up in a steam of feeling and read the *Gazette* again, ordered a *Courier* for a month, called at the confectioner's and read all the papers till I was faint. . . . 'Have not the efforts of the nation', I asked myself 'been gigantic? To such glories, she only wants to add the glories of my noble art to make her the grandest nation in the world, and these she shall have if God spare my life.'

"June 25: Read the *Gazette* again, till I now know it actually by heart. Dined with Hunt. I give myself great credit for not worrying him to death at this news; he was quiet for some time, but knowing it must come by-and-by, and putting on an air of indifference, he said, 'Terrible battle this, Haydon.' 'A glorious one, Hunt.' 'Oh, yes, certainly', and to it we went.

"Yet Hunt took a just and liberal view of the question. As for Hazlitt, it is not to be believed how the destruction of Napoleon affected him; he seemed prostrated in mind and body, he walked about unwashed, unshaved, hardly sober by day, and always intoxicated by night, literally, without exaggeration, for weeks; until at length, wakening up as it were from his stupor, he at once left off all stimulating liquors, and never touched them after."

Hazlitt, who wrote a vast biography of Napoleon, simply could not adapt to the destruction of his idol. Not being an imaginative writer, he has left us no record of his inner struggles and sufferings. But his story is useful as background to that of a great poet who endured all this and *has* left an account of it. The young Wordsworth toured France during the first heady, idealistic days of the Revolution, when every café and every town square was the forum for excited debate, when new ideas were springing up everywhere and "human nature seeming born again."

And when revolutionary France became Napoleonic France, and entered on her expansionist phase, Wordsworth's agony was deep; a country boy, rooted in his environment and his neighbourhood, he could not make the effortless switch to supporting a foreign power against his own country, to cheering on soldiers who were killing his countrymen, that came so easily to the rootless Viet Nam generation.

> . . .I, who with the breeze
> Had play'd, a green leaf on the blessed tree
> Of my beloved country; nor had wish'd
> For happier fortune than to wither there,
> Now from my pleasant station was cut off,
> And toss'd about in whirlwinds. I rejoiced,
> Yea, afterwards, truth most painful to record!
> Exulted in the triumph of my soul
> When Englishmen by thousands were o'erthrown,
> Left without glory on the Field, or driven,
> Brave hearts, to shameful flight. It was a grief,
> Grief call it not, 'twas anything but that,
> A conflict of sensations without name,
> Of which he only who may love the sight
> Of a Village Steeple as I do can judge
> When in the Congregation, bending all
> To their great Father, prayers were offer'd up,
> Or praises for our Country's Victories,
> And 'mid the simple worshippers, perchance,
> I only, like an uninvited Guest
> Whom no one own'd sate silent, shall I add,
> Fed on the day of vengeance yet to come?

There is the note of tragedy, too, in his description of France under the Terror, when blood-lust attacked the nation like a plague, and "the crimes of few Became the madness of the many." These passages remind us that there is nothing anti-poetic, anti-imaginative, in public affairs as such. All that is needful — but it is totally and at all times needful — is that the situation should claim the poet entirely, down to the roots of his being and come up as fresh foliage; there must be no parading with boughs cut from Birnam Wood.

The wave of populism that is washing over our society at the moment is an interesting phenomenon and deserves to be analysed calmly. One of its most striking features, when we come to any of the arts, is the deep-seated guilt about privilege, the feeling that what all can't have, no one must. This has now reached the proportions of a mania. The other day I noticed someone airing his views in a correspondence column, maintaining that the Oxford Union, to whose usefulness as a training-ground several politicians had been testifying, was "a private, privileged club" which should be abolished immediately. Setting aside the question of whether the Union is useful to an aspiring politician or merely misleading — I wouldn't know — it still seems worth pausing for a moment over this notion of privilege. The society is open to anyone who becomes a member of Oxford University and is willing to pay a modest subscription; thousands of young people become eligible for membership every year and continue to be eligible as long as they live; if this is "privilege", then so is everything that can't be joined by any casual passer-by in the street. Hasn't every school, every university, every regiment, every lodge, every Trade Union, some organisation that is restricted to its own membership — if only for mere manageability's sake? But we must breathe fire and slaughter over the Oxford Union Society because (I suppose) the word "Oxford" has the same resonance as the word "privilege" in its emotional field, and because Conservative (as well as Socialist) politicians acknowledge a debt to it.

Enough of this Aunt Sally game at three shies a penny. But the unimportant straw shows the direction of an important wind. It is this wind that makes young poets afraid to study their craft with any real professional devotion, lest their writing should appear to be losing that cherished note of the casual and the familiar, the four-letter and the street-corner, which is its party card. Back — or forward, or sideways — to a folk idiom! And the interest in folk art is in itself sympathetic, possibly even fruitful. Except that underneath it one scents a fallacy, a sentimental impulse to pretend. The fact is that the cult of folk art, in "developed" countries, is exactly on a par with the cult of the steam traction engine. It is nostalgic; it warms itself by keeping alive the memory of something kindly, and slow, and old-fashioned. The crowds at folk-concerts, the crowds at cosy, slangy poetry-readings, are indulging in nostalgia — which isn't, in itself, a sin; it only becomes hampering when it obscures a clear-sighted view of the situation. And the situation is that the folk idiom is dead. As soon as there is a popular press, let alone radio, film, television, then folk art lies with a dagger in its heart. And if we try to imitate a folk idiom, to put flesh and skin on those dead bones by an act of will, we are condemning ourselves to an art without roots.

The fact is that any poet who wants to work at the most effective level, to realise the power of his own imagination, and to communicate with the greatest number of people, will use the full resources of modern poetry as they have been developed, internationally, by experimentation and study. The "difficult" modern poet, whose work is supposed to be unintelligible and is anathema to the populist, ends up being read by a much wider public than the *faux-naïf* or even the genuine *naïf*.

True, there is a perfectly reasonable counter-argument to this. The modern arts command a large public because they offer work in a bourgeois idiom and they address a bourgeois audience. Since most of the people who expect to take any notice of art — to go to concerts, to buy books, to frequent art galleries — are middle-class, they naturally attend to the middle-class artist. And since these are the people who travel abroad, study foreign languages, attend international universities, and so forth, the bourgeois artist is addressing a large international public, able to dispose of large funds; sometimes privately, sometimes by influencing the channelling of public money. All this, we are assured, will be different when we have changed the structure of society and abolished the class system.

So be it. In an utterly changed society, there will be an utterly changed art, just as there will be utterly changed conceptions of justice, leisure, and productivity. Perhaps even happiness and sadness will change their character, as they seem to have done already in the hippie jungles. But — to use an expression from the common tongue that was already well-worn when Jonathan Swift overheard it and transferred it to the printed page — let us not throw out our dirty water till we get clean. It would be a tragic mistake to abandon a tradition of art and literature that is still sound and fruitful, merely because it can be hastily stigmatised as "bourgeois". It is, doubtless, a thing to be regretted that the bourgeois person takes an interest in art and invests time and effort in appreciating it and the manual worker doesn't — but we shall not remedy that state of affairs just by ridiculing the bourgeois until he gives up and turns his time and effort elsewhere. Thus leaving "the field" clear — what field?

The bourgeoisie, as at present constituted, has one great redeeming feature as a public for art. It numbers many people who are not, or not totally and all the time, politicised. It contains many individuals who can look at a work of art simply as an utterance on behalf of general humanity, without asking whether it can be narrowed down to serve this or that Cause. Not that Causes aren't important, but their importance is not the same as that of art.

Any why in the end, does it matter so much? Why do we take so much trouble to protect art from the meaty hands of those whose wish is to grab it, package it, weigh and measure it, twist it into a shape convenient for their purposes and then another shape and another, till they tire of it at last and throw it out with the other broken toys? Why not let them have it?

We cannot let them have it because art, the free exercise of the imagination, is just about the only thing we have left, the only complete success our species can point to. Most of our techniques concern pure bedrock survival. But if we want to do more than survive, if we want to lift up our heads and assert that we, too, amount to something, what is there left but art? Everything else is a failure or a compromise. Men of science toil devotedly for years, breaking through time after time into fresh knowledge, and at the end of it their discoveries are absorbed into a technology that devises crueller and crueller weapons, that puts three men on the moon while three million starve for want of common bread. Politicians make power-structures which, at the most, give security and contentment to a bare majority. The most successful form of government is sixty per cent failure, if the object of government is to give people happiness and justice; and over most of the world's surface, government is simply another name for bloody terror and exploitation.

Turn to the inward life and the same picture is there. Mystics may be exalted but they cannot pass on their exaltation to their fellow-men; saints are imperfect and are tortured by their imperfection; every attempt at a life has failed. Others again base their ideal of fulfilment on personal relationships, and shrivel into dust at the first betrayal, which comes sooner or later as surely as the leaves fall off the trees. Only in the sphere of art is humanity able to rise totally above its failures and inadequacies. Contemplating a great painting, listening to a great symphony, watching a great play, reading a great novel or poem, only then are we in the presence of the human assertion without the human denial, the human achievement without the human failure, the human splendour without the human tarnish — if only because the denial, the failure, the tarnish, are taken into that totality and orchestrated with it, and lifted up, so that we see our imperfections mirrored in our splendours, and we accept ourselves, at last, in peace and thankfulness. The glories of art are the only totally achieved glories we have left; and to the people who want always to cheapen them, to bring them down into the committee-room and the parade-ground, who want to use them as a means and muzzle them and discipline them and chop them into convenient lengths, our answer must be the same as it has been for hundreds of years, the only possible answer, the answer that is given in the closing words of *Love's Labour's Lost* —

The words of Mercury are harsh after the songs of Apollo: you that way, we this way.

Encounter

The business of establishing authentic texts is a branch of literary studies which has arguably made greater advances than any other in the 20th century. On the question of the principles upon which texts should be established, there has of course been strenuous debate between, on the one hand, the bibliographers and textual critics with their scientific and mechanical procedures, and, on the other, champions of literary judgment. Nevertheless the assumption that it is vital to determine exactly what words a given author wrote is shared by all parties.

This assumption does not arise from any conviction that the right reading will be the most appealing. The textual critic's personal taste is irrelevant. To rediscover the text is his aim, not to improve it. Our craving for authenticity in this respect arises from a relatively modern consciousness of the indissoluble fusion of form and content in a work of literature. It is a fusion, we now take it for granted, so subtle and profound that the terms 'form' and 'content' have themselves come to seem coarse and obsolete — no longer acceptable elements in a critic's vocabulary, since they insist upon a separation in which we no longer believe.

The relative modernity of this view strikes us with especial clarity when we glance back at an early English critic like Dryden, in whom we find a precisely contrary assumption. Dryden believed not only that form and content were divisible but that, even in the best authors, the form might well benefit from a drastic overhaul which would leave the content unimpaired. Thus in the preface to his adaptation of Shakespeare's *Troilus and Cressida* Dryden first lists what seem to him the play's shortcomings, and then continues: 'Yet, after all, because the play was Shakespeare's, and that there appeared in some places of it the admirable genius of the author, I undertook to remove that heap of rubbish under which many excellent thoughts lay wholly buried.' The heap of rubbish here referred to includes Shakespeare's language, in particular his imagery, which Dryden found overdone and obscure.

The earliest spokesman for our modern view of the intimate bond between text and meaning was Coleridge, who records in the *Biographia Literaria* that, by reading and meditation, he came to realise that it would be scarcely more difficult to push a stone out from the pyramids with the bare hand than to alter a word, or the position of a word, in Milton or Shakespeare (in their most important works at least), without making the author say something else, or something worse, than he does say.

No modern critic would dissent from that. We take it as an axiom that paraphrase inevitably alters meaning. To reword is to destroy.

I labour the point about paraphase only because its implications for the practice of literary criticism seem to me to have been rather curiously overlooked. For a glance through any representative selection of the books and articles which literary critics have turned out so plentifully during the last half-century will be enough to convince one that what the writers are, for much of the time, busily engaged upon is rewording the literary texts about which they are writing. And since literature cannot conceivably be reworded without destroying its meaning, it follows the literary critics spend much of their time destroying the meaning of literature.

This is an unpleasant conclusion, and may not be accepted without some exemplification. However, since the practice I am referring to is so widespread, examples are not hard to find. They thrust themselves upon the reader, indeed, in embarrassing quantities, and the only problem is selection. Four instances of rewording will both make clear the sort of thing I have in mind and enable anyone interested to pick out plenty of kindred instances from his own experience of literary criticism.

The first is from Empson's *Seven Types of Ambiguity,* probably the most important seminal work in English criticism this century, and one that is almost entirely composed of rewordings and re-rewordings of pieces of literature. One could pick an instance from anywhere in this book and I have taken mine, more or less at random, from Chapter VI where Empson is discussing Herbert's poem 'Affliction', in particular the famous and paradoxical prayer at the end of that poem: 'Ah, my dear God, though I am clean forgot,/Let me not love thee, if I love thee not.' Empson tries out various rewordings of the last line which, he says, can be made 'grammatical and sensible' only if we assume a distinction of meaning between the two uses of the word 'love'. Perhaps, he suggests, Herbert really wants to stop loving God: he is asking to be released from the effort of trying to love God in some special, mystical way which has eluded him. For this meaning Empson offers the paraphrase: 'Do not let me spend my life trying to love you, loving you in will and deed but not in the calm of which so few are worthy.' Alternatively, Empson acknowledges, Herbert may be affirming that he does love God (as the apostrophe 'Ah, my dear God' plainly suggests). The poet chooses the worst imprecation he can think of for the first half of the line – 'Let me not love thee' – in order to give force to his determination to go on loving. For this meaning Empson offers the paraphase: 'Damn me if I don't stick to the parsonage.'

The motive behind this crude rewording is not hard to fathom. Empson wants to deter his readers from the way of understanding the line that will probably have occurred to them, and accordingly he reduces it to a comic paraphrase so that they will feel ashamed of thinking the line meant that, and be readier to believe Empson's less likely alternative. In a footnote to later editions of *Seven Types* Empson records that F. L. Lucas took this treatment of Herbert's poem as proof of the vulgarity of his approach, and he adds in excuse: 'No doubt it is flippantly written, but a purely logical point can be made more clearly if it is not muffled by a sympathetic tone.' We notice here the two assumptions that a 'purely logical point' may appropriately be made about the meaning of a poem, and that a paraphrase may be better if it misrepresents the poem's tone. In both assumptions, Empson has had a large following. Not that 'Damn me if I don't stick to the parsonage' seems much worse than the flabby prose of Empson's other rewording: 'Do not let me spend my life trying to love you, loving you in will and deed but not in the calm of which so few are worthy.' Herbert's poem happily says nothing about 'the calm of which so few are worthy', and if we accept such a phrase, along with 'Damn me if I don't stick to the parsonage', as part of our experience in reading the poem, we are rewording and therefore destroying it.

The second example also shows paraphrase being used to destroy the reader's view of what is before his eyes, though the motive is rather different. It is taken from the section on Spenser's *Faerie Queene* in C. S. Lewis's *The Allegory of Love,* and the bit which I should like to draw attention to is Lewis's account of the two naked damsels who 'wrestle wantonly' in a fountain, and whom Guyon comes upon during his visit to Acrasia's Bower of Bliss. Here, to remind us of Spenser's version, is his description of the girls' reaction when they see Guyon:

> *The wanton Maidens, him espying stood*
> *Gazing awhile at his unwonted guise;*
> *Then th' one her selfe low ducked in the flood,*
> *Abasht that her a straunger did avise;*
> *But thother rather higher did arise,*
> *And her two lilly paps aloft displayd,*
> *And all that might his melting hart entyse*
> *To her delights she unto him bewrayd;*
> *The rest hidd underneath him more desirous made . . .*
>
> *Withall she laughed, and she blusht withall,*
> *That blushing to her laughter gave more grace,*
> *And laughter to her blushing, as did fall.*

Lewis is anxious that the immorality of the girls' behaviour should not escape us, and he comments:

> Here, I presume, no one can be confused. Acrasia's two young women (their names are obviously Cissie and Flossie) are ducking and giggling in a bathing-pool for the benefit of a passer-by: a man does not need to go to faerie land to meet them.

Unfortunately he does not divulge where one might go to meet them. But his gratuitous introduction of what are presumably meant to be lower-class names — Cissie and Flossie — leaves one with the impression that they are very much the sort of thing a man might have to brace himself to encounter on his way through the poorer districts between Magdalen College and Headington. At all events, some sort of class point is being made, and it is important to realise that it is utterly alien to Spenser's wording, as is the implication that the girls can be easily contemned. They are, on the contrary, exquisitely beautiful. The interflow of blushing and laughter in the last three lines I quoted, suggesting the colour coming and going in the girl's face, is one of the triumphs of Spenser's verbal art, and if we can read it and fail to see that no word could be changed without damage, we are not fit to read it. Lewis's word, 'giggling', is Lewis's word, not Spenser's. And Lewis's bluff certitude — 'Here, I presume, no one can be confused' — is entirely misplaced, for Guyon, as Spenser shows us, *is* confused, and successfully enticed by the girls, until the Palmer interposes. That sexual temptation can be readily shrugged off, and that only Cissies and Flossies would try it on, are simpler and more optimistic conclusions than any Spenser allows us. Lewis's rewording, as rewording must, has destroyed Spenser's meaning.

On the other hand he had, one might say, the best intentions. Unlike Empson, who merely wanted to distract his readers' attention from an obvious meaning, Lewis had, as always, his readers' welfare at heart, and was concerned lest they should have impure thoughts. He took steps to make the poetry less seductive accordingly. My third specimen is also from a critic who has virtuous, if misleading, intentions. It occurs in Christopher Ricks's discussion of the ending of Milton's *Samson Agonistes* where Milton's Samson, like the Samson of Judges, pulls down the theatre upon the heads of the unsuspecting Philistine audience. 'Why is Samson's pulling down of the pillars,' asks Ricks, 'not . . . a merely brutal act of revenge? . . . There are limits to what a *donnée* in great literature can be asked to encompass, and genocide is beyond them.' The word 'genocide' is here superimposed upon, or rather substituted for, the 200 lines of dramatic verse which Milton has used to organise and control our response to the catastrophe. 'Genocide' brings vividly to mind the racial atrocities of the 20th century, and invites us to equate these with what Milton is writing about. As a piece of rewording it is more powerful and destructive than the previous two examples, since its tendency is to make us feel morally superior to Milton.

There are two procedures, I think, which might be adopted in rejecting Ricks's paraphrase. One, the more conventional and straightforward, would be to point out that it is, as it happens, not accurate. It distorts the issues as presented both in Judges and in Milton's drama. The reason for Samson's destruction of the Philistines is not that they are Philistines but that they are tyrants. Not their race, but their unjust oppression of Samson's people, the Israelites, brings down vengeance upon them. Should we wish to substitute a technical term for Samson's deed — which we don't — it would have to be tyrannicide, not genocide. Milton believed in a people's right to destroy tyrants, which is why he justified the execution of Charles in his

Defence of the English People. In that work he actually alludes to Samson as a model, observing that Samson 'thought it not impious but pious to kill those masters who were tyrants over his country'.

That Samson is killing masters, tyrants, is emphasised, too, by an unprecedented change which Milton makes in the biblical account, a change which does not fit in with Ricks's view, and which he omits to mention. Recounting Samson's deed, the messenger reports that those who were killed were only the Philistines' political, military and religious leaders — 'Lords, ladies, captains, counsellors, or priests'. The common people, since they did not qualify for the best seats, were not harmed: 'The vulgar only scaped who stood without.' It was Milton's own idea: the Bible account makes no such exception. 'Genocide', then — 'the deliberate and systematic extermination of an ethnic or national group' — far from being an appropriate rewording of Milton, is a term which could as accurately be applied to the execution of the Nazi war criminals as it could to Samson's destruction of the tyrannous rulers who have deprived the Jewish people of their liberty.

That, as I say, is one sort of argument for rejecting Ricks's paraphrase. But the other, equally forceful, would be to reject it simply on the grounds that it *is* paraphrase: to insist with Coleridge that it would be scarcely more difficult to push a stone out from the pyramids with the bare hand than to alter a word in Milton or Shakespeare without making the author say something else, or something worse, than he does say; and that therefore, even supposing 'genocide' did bear a more accurate relation to the facts behind Milton's drama than it does, it would still be misconceived to intrude it into, or substitute it for, the particular experience with its precise ebbs and flows of feeling, its excitement of some parts of our being and suppression of others, which Milton has been at pains for 200 lines to create. Once the rewording — 'genocide' — is admitted as a part of our response, what Milton has created is destroyed.

The three critics quoted from so far are, needless to say, exceptionally distinguished. I have deliberately chosen figures of such eminence — Empson, Lewis, Ricks — to forestall the retort that the destruction of literature is an activity popular only among the second-rate. But there is a disadvantage in confining oneself to such exemplars, for their very intelligence makes them unrepresentative. It inhibits them from giving way to the desperate ingenuity which accounts for a large proportion of the rewording endemic among literary critics. My fourth specimen has been selected to illustrate this, and is taken from a recent book, *The Prophetic Milton*, by an American critic, William Kerrigan.

Kerrigan, like Ricks, is interested in the ending of *Samson Agonistes*. However, in his account what takes place there is not genocide but something more medical. His attention is attracted by the repeated references to wind — Manoa saying, 'What windy joy this day had I conceived', and Samson tugging down the pillars 'As with the force of winds and waters pent'. Samson, Kerrigan deduces, is in fact suffering from wind, or symbolic wind, and between the pillars he is able to get rid of it:

> Samson purges all the bile, rancor, fester, gangrene, rage and mortification of the mind. He does so in the posture of relieved constipation, 'straining' and 'bow'd', the release coming 'with horrible convulsion' and at last 'with burst of thunder'.

Attached as he is to this rewording, Kerrigan also feels that Samson, between the pillars, is giving birth, or perhaps being born, besides alleviating his constipation. He has, after all, been 'labouring' at the mill, and he feels 'rousing motions' which, Kerrigan suggests, may be 'the great rhythms of the mother' asserting themselves, as well as Samson's bowels moving. The result, Kerrigan curiously explains, is an instance of those 'births that emerge as anal discharges', and upon this association of excretion and birth depends, he concludes 'the significance of the climactic moment between the pillars'.

Now although it is impossible not to feel dismay as one watches Kerrigan destroying the end of *Samson Agonistes,* it is also, unless one has been remarkably secluded from modern literary criticism, impossible to feel much surprise. Most of us could, no doubt, cite scores of examples of criticism just as resolutely perverse, just as adept at seizing upon a few words and phrases from the text, distorting their significance, ignoring their context, and, through the combined exertions of zeal, muddle and insensitivity, popping up with a brand new interpretation. Kerrigan would probably concede that *Samson Agonistes* loses dignity and elevation as a result of his emphasis — but some sacrifice, he might reply, is bound to be involved if literary critics are to keep discovering new meanings for works that have already been pored over for centuries. The new meanings will inevitably stretch one's credulity a little, for the credible ones have all been used up.

These, then, are my four examples — Empson, Ricks, Lewis, Kerrigan. You will notice that each rewords for a different purpose, and that taken together the four purposes account for a large amount of the literary criticism currently produced. Ricks rewords to subvert, and establish his ethical superiority to the work under examination; Lewis, on the contrary, rewords to hammer home what he takes to be his work's ethical aim. Empson rewords to fend his readers off from an interpretation they might have thought of for themselves; Kerrigan to entrammel them in one which no reader in his senses could possibly have thought of unaided.

To my allegation that the energies of literary critics are regularly expended in rewording, one or two objections might be made. First it might be pleaded that what these critics are doing is commenting or glossing rather than rewording, and that despite their efforts the text itself remains unharmed. To this I should reply that, in the first place, this does not distinguish them from Dryden rewriting *Troilus and Cressida*, since he too left Shakespeare's text unharmed in the sense that the reader could still refer back to it. He simply supposed that his own words were true to the meaning of the original, just as these critics do, and by supposing that, he abrogated the claim of that original to be the only possible wording of its meaning — a claim upon which, as I have said, our whole modern understanding of literary form is based. And further I should question what is meant by leaving a text unharmed. If we accept 'genocide' or 'Cissie and Flossie' or 'constipation' as parts of the meaning of the texts — that is, if we remember those words at all when reading the texts — then the texts will not be unharmed but disfigured. The original words will receive a colouring not imparted by the literary works themselves, much as if a distorting film had been slipped across the reader's eye.

On the other hand, if we do not remember the critics' words when reading the texts, then what, we may ask, is the point of reading the critics in the first place? We arrive at the paradoxical conclusion that only criticism which can be instantly forgotten is safe to read — or that this is so, at any rate, where criticism consists of rewording. Not that there is any shortage of instantly forgettable criticism, of course. The danger comes from the good critics, since they can permanently alter the way readers see a piece of work, and alter it in a way which the work itself does not sanction.

A second objection that might be made to my case is that my examples, distinguished as they are, are too flagrant to be typical. Certainly they are, in their way, more notable than much of the rewording that currently goes on, though that scarcely seems to me grounds for feeling happy about the general situation. One impulse which produces critical rewording thick and fast, and which I have not exemplified because it would be too dull and anyway cannot have escaped observation, is the impulse to moralise. Novels, plays, poems, which present human predicaments in all their complexity, present truth, as it is truth's way to be, 'Flexible, changeable, vague, and multiform and doubtful', and present it through obliquities of narrative and dramatic method that compound its life-giving uncertainties — such works are flattened by the moralisers into little homogenised pellets of abstraction which they will, seemingly without a qualm, pass off as the 'meaning' of the literature under inspection. Hence the drab cavalcade of articles and books on Shakespeare or Dickens — to name only two authors who have suffered at the hands of the moralisers — which announce the meanings of the masterpieces they have fixed upon in terms of appearance versus reality, or the dangers of passion, or the need for love, or the capitalist ethic, or some kindred platitude, so that the reader is put to wondering why these critics, if they find such formulations satisfactory, have ever bothered with literature at all, unless it be that literature by its very multiplicity and lawlessness provokes them to beat it into shape and destroy it. This impulse is a particular temptation, it seems, to academic critics. Committed as they are to organising literature and turning it into a discipline, they readily come to believe that the function of literature is to propound doctrines of moral and social utility, and from that it is a short step to extracting such doctrines in clearer language for their pupils' use.

A third and different kind of hostile response to my contention would be to demand: 'What else can critics do? Unless they are to be restricted simply to quoting the works they are discussing, how can they help using new words, and pretending that they serve the same purpose as the original words, even though they know that with every new word something of the work's meaning will have been destroyed?' One alternative open to them is, of course, silence. Nor do I suggest this flippantly. No one, least of all university teachers of English, can feel much elation about the volume of literary criticism available at present. The subject has shown a capacity for growth rather than progress. For progress would discard outmoded criticism. Whereas in fact no sooner is it outmoded than it becomes part of the Critical Heritage, and so a requisite component of study. Thus the pile of secondary matter separating students from literature grows yearly more daunting, and undergraduates are inclined either to limit themselves to modern authors, on whom the critics have not yet gathered so thickly, or to pick some tiny period from the past in which they can specialise: that is, read all the worthless rewordings that present themselves. The sort of industry that produces, say, a volume entitled *44 Essential Articles on Pope* spells death to English studies, if only because the multiplication of such volumes will leave less and less time for reading Pope. Indeed, the discredit into which literature itself has already fallen can be gauged from the changed attitude towards memorising passages of it. Nowadays candidates in the Oxford English School are issued with a text of Shakespeare in the examination room, to indicate that actually remembering what words Shakespeare used, and in what order, would be to squander time that might be more profitably spent. Meanwhile simplified rewordings of literature are increasingly produced for students, so that the literary works themselves come to seem annoyingly elaborate versions of what is put more plainly in the Reader's Guide.

In order to eschew rewording, it is necessary for literary criticism to develop an acuter sense of what literary criticism can't do. And in this respect it might learn from literature itself. For one of the perennial strengths of literature is that it retains an awareness of its own shortcomings, an acknowledgement of the health and validity of experiences that lie beyond literature's — beyond language's — grasp. There is a poem of Robert Graves called 'The Cool Web' which is relevant here and which, distrusting paraphrase, I shall quote from:

> *Children are dumb to say how hot the day is,*
> *How hot the scent is of the summer rose,*
> *How dreadful the black wastes of evening sky,*
> *How dreadful the tall soldiers drumming by.*

> *But we have speech, to chill the angry day,*
> *And speech, to dull the rose's cruel scent.*
> *We spell away the overhanging night,*
> *We spell away the soldiers and the fright.*
>
> *There's a cool web of language winds us in,*
> *Retreat from too much joy or too much fear . . .*

Associated with what Graves concedes here is literature's willingness to admit literature's complicity in delusion and in substitutes for living, and to admit, on the other hand, the strengths of the unliterary – a willingness which we can trace in literature from Don Quixote to Leopold Bloom.

Modelling itself on literature in this respect, criticism might become more tolerant of the uncritical, readier to acknowledge the importance of the feeling, induced by great works of literature, that there is nothing more to be said: that words have made any further words insufferable: that words are, indeed, the one thing the critic cannot use – as the sculptor's chisel, when it has completed its work, makes the intrusion of anyone else's chisel an act of vandalism. At the same time criticism might develop some wholesome self-doubt about the state of mind which is appropriate to the reading of literature. It seems frequently to be assumed, for instance (and here Empson comes to mind once more), that all poetry is best approached in a mood of keen logicality. Critics can be found denouncing poets for not conforming to their own standards of commonsense observation, whereas it might have struck them, one feels, that it is precisely that failure in conformity that makes the poets poets and the critics merely critics.

An instance of this tendency might be taken from Leavis's essay on Shelley, where Leavis is expressing his dissatisfaction with some lines from the *Ode to the West Wind:*

> *Thou on whose stream, mid the steep sky's commotion,*
> *Loose clouds like earth's decaying leaves are shed,*
> *Shook from the tangled boughs of Heaven and Ocean.*
> *Angels of rain and lightning . . .*

Upon which Leavis comments:

> The sweeping movement of the verse, with the accompanying plangency, is so potent that, as many can testify, it is possible to have been for years familiar with the Ode − to know it by heart − without asking the obvious questions. In what respects are the 'loose clouds' like 'decaying leaves'? The correspondence is certainly not in shape, colour or way of moving. It is only the vague general sense of windy tumult that associates the clouds and the leaves . . . What again, are those 'tangled boughs of Heaven and Ocean'? They stand for nothing that Shelley could have pointed to in the scene before him.

To which our only response can be, why ever should they? And why ever should Shelley's association of clouds and leaves be reducible to the categories of shape, colour and way of moving, or be susceptible to any such analytic rewording as Leavis appears to require? That Shelley's wording has created a fusion of clouds and leaves is testified by the fact that it has satisfied, as Leavis acknowledges, generations of readers. A critic who finds that he cannot respond, as these readers have responded, proclaims an inadequacy in himself, not in the poem. And a critic who complains because a poet's words do not correspond to anything he can point to in the scene before him betrays a strange misapprehension about our reasons for needing imaginative literature.

In the conduct of such pugnacious analytic sallies against literature, a phrase that has appealed to some academic critics is 'the primacy of meaning'. By insisting that they are committed to 'the primacy of meaning', by which they mean the primacy of paraphrasable content, critics are able to save themselves the trouble of accounting for the power of those parts of literature, such as the sound and rhythm of the words, which are notoriously the most difficult to discuss rationally. These elements − the elements which Leavis refers to in his Shelley piece as 'the sweeping movement of the verse, with the accompanying plangency' − can, once 'the primacy of meaning' has been invoked, be discarded as allurements, hung out to catch the fancy of less discriminating readers, while the critic, more trenchant and demanding, strips away the cosmetic shell and bears off in triumph the poem's meaning − or rather, a little heap of his own phrases which he imagines to be equivalent to that meaning. Often, of course, he will see that the little heap is composed of rather disappointing material, but instead of blaming his own procedures, he will vilify the poem for containing nothing more worthwhile, and for failing to measure up to 'the primacy of meaning'. 'The primacy of meaning' is certainly a phrase that would have delighted Dryden, who felt that that was just what he was trying to bring out when he deleted the poetic imagery from *Troilus and Cressida*.

But since, as we have agreed, no word or position of a word can be altered in a piece of literature without destroying its meaning, it follows that the primacy of meaning means nothing but the primacy of the whole text. Literature *means* with all and every part of its being and there can be no justification for allocating a superior status to those parts of it which can be isolated by the reasoning faculty. Such a course is convenient for the literary critic, since literary criticism is generally (or generally purports to be) a reasoning medium. But it is purely arbitrary, much as if a non-swimmer were to proclaim the 'primacy' of dry land.

It seems to me, then, that it is a paramount duty of the literary critic not merely not to reword himself, but to contest and discredit all rewordings fabricated by other critics, demonstrating their inadequacy and destructiveness. In this way he will be, if you like, an anti-critic rather than a critic, but he will, by this activity, persistently bear witness to the fact that literature is irreplaceable, irreducible and quite distinct in its mode of being from literary criticism.

A further duty, finally, will be to rebuild for the reader, as far as possible, the context — linguistic, social, biographical — within which any given piece of literature originally existed. For seen outside that context it can be only a botched replica, reshaped and reworded by an alien culture. Some critics despise this historical effort, of course, and attempt to discredit it by pointing out that we can never, in fact, enter a past consciousness. To slough off decades or centuries of discovery, and put ourselves into the skin and mind of an Elizabethan or Victorian reader is, they argue, patently impossible, a game of let's-pretend played with a broken-down time-machine.

The argument does not, I think, carry the weight that its proponents imagine. That to enter completely into the consciousness of another era, as of another human being, is impossible, is perfectly true. But in what field of human endeavour is complete success possible? We do not forsake the practice of medicine because we cannot keep people alive for ever. To realise how hard one must strive for even a partial historical understanding is in itself more educative than remaining in ignorance, since it brings us up against the limiting nature of our preconceptions. And if it is asked, why should we try — why should we not treat literature as cultural plasticine, responsive to our contemporary pressures? — the answer must be that this is ultimately the same question as, why should we object to rewording literature? Empson, at the end of *Seven Types,* favoured the plasticine approach: 'It is the business of the critic,' he wrote, 'to extract for his public what it wants; to organise, what he may indeed create, the taste of his period.' The trouble with this is that it allows critic and public no chance of escaping *from* their period, and so no chance of criticising it from the standpoint of other cultures. Yet this is the only way our own culture can be criticised. To criticise it from within is ineffective, because then we are restricted to those values and responses which our period has itself fashioned. The public given, in Empson's phrase, 'what it wants', will remain locked in its standard reactions, and it will reword literature to fit these. Fortunately, as I have tried to show, literature resists such treatment. For books, as Milton reminds us, 'are not absolutely dead things'. A book, *Areopagitica* asserts, is 'the precious life-blood of a master-spirit, embalmed and treasured up on purpose to a life beyond life'. Blood, like literature — and unlike plasticine — can give life, because it comes from another organism, another life, distinct from and as real as our own. By not rewording we pay the due tribute to that distinctness and that reality. By learning to know that other life we both escape from and enlarge our own identity: we grow, as selves, because other selves flow into us, and add their strengths and weaknesses, their ways of knowing and not knowing, to our own. 'We live' — if I may finish by quoting from Randall Jarrell's poem, 'Children Selecting Books in a Library':

> *We live*
> *By trading another's sorrow for our own, another's*
> *Impossibilities, still unbelieved in, for our own . . .*
> *'I am myself still'? For a little while, forget:*
> *The world's selves cure that short disease, myself . . .*

New Statesman

Poems from Books and Pamphlets
1976-1977

Peter Bland   **On Government Lawns**

Fat peasants hurl their Gucci Bags
in the face of the press. Country
cousins are new here. They'll soon learn.
Only last year they were dressed in rags
and crawling across parched·fields. How
elegant the generals' wives are! And
the generals themselves are trying so hard
to be decent and well-bred. At least
one can't hear the screams in the palace yard
above the massed murmur of string quartets.
And the doves are lovely. (Except the dead ones.)
Whole container-trucks full of peace! In
the gardens a coven of past presidents
are playing golf with some refugees.
How happy the old statesmen are
now that the assassins are somewhere else!
They wave their clubs and weep. They're
like children really. They only
want to be revered. In a rush
of patriotism at the champagne bar
two bodyguards shoot each other
through the knees. It's a farce of course
but on such a scale! When the handshakes cease
bodies are piled up house-high in the streets.

Mr. Maui London Magazine Editions

Peter Bland   **This Way to Samarkand**

Whenever I'm broke and grubbing around
for the price of a pint, I think
of James Elroy Flecker who wrote

anything to pay the bills —
tourists blurbs, trade journal guff —
writing it with a will and in
a white shirt because that way
he might get hired again. Not
a popular man (having no influence)
and a bit of a stay-at-home — but
in the few hours that he won for himself
then to hell with bangers and mash and
yahoo to the local literati! Keeping
his head in the clouds he built
the entire city of Samarkand. No-one
knocked on those doors with a bailiff!
And so, whenever I'm broke, I join
James Elroy on his elephant-clouds
heading east over the roofs of the town
with the sunlight streaming through our empty hands
and our wives and children swaying at the back.

Mr Maui London Magazine Editions

Ciarán Carson   **To A Married Sister**

Helping you to move in, unpacking,
I was proudly shown the bedroom. Patches
Of damp stained the wall a tea colour,
Like the sluggish tints of an old map.
Our mother would have said, 'A new bride
And a through-other house make a bad match',

But you like dilapidation, the touch
Of somewhere that's been lived-in — the gloom
Of empty hallways, the shadow of the fanlight
Fading dimly, imperceptibly
Along the flowered paper; the hairline net
Of cracks on worn enamel; a tree-darkened room.

I left you cluttered with gifts — crockery,
Knives, the bed-linen still in its cellophane —
Watching you in that obscure privacy
Pick your way through the white delf
And golden straw to trace your new initials
On the spidered window-pane.

Your husband had talked of mending
Broken doors, the cheap furniture
That bore the accidents of others' lives,
That were there before you. A gold resin
Leaked from the slackened joints.
His new saw glittered like your wedding-silver.

The New Estate Blackstaff Press (Belfast)

45

Ciarán Carson   **Soot**

It was autumn. First, she shrouded
The furniture, then rolled back the carpet
As if for dancing; then moved
The ornaments from the mantelpiece,
Afraid his roughness might disturb
Their staid fragility.

He came: shyly, she let him in,
Feeling ill-at-ease in the newly-spacious
Room, her footsteps sounding hollow
On the boards. She watched him kneel
Before the hearth, and said something
About the weather. He did not answer,

Too busy with his work for speech.
The stem of yellow cane creaked upwards
Tentatively. After a while, he asked
Her to go outside and look; and there,
Above the roof, she saw the frayed sunflower
Bloom triumphantly. She came back,

And asked how much she owed him, grimacing
As she put the money in his soiled hand.
When he had gone, a weightless hush
Lingered in the house for days. Slowly,
It settled; the fire burned cleanly;
Everything was spotless.

Hearing that soot was good for the soil,
She threw it on the flowerbeds. She would watch
It crumble, dissolving in the rain,
Finding its way to lightless crevices,
Sleeping, till in spring it would emerge softly
As the ink-bruise in the pansy's heart.

The New Estate Blackstaff Press (Belfast)

Gladys Mary Coles   **Hour Glass**

Consider the shape of an hour glass —
the constant flow
from rounded upper to rounded lower,
the balance held
in that narrow channel-span
where falls each individual grain
from the full and crystal bowl
inevitably to the waiting lower sphere,
and every falling grain
the total sand receives.
Shape of glass to corresponding glass,
lower to upper, and again the same.

Consider the sands of an hour glass,
creating their own tide
which knows no late or soon,
which cannot wash away
or cover the shells,
obeys no moon.

The Sounding Circle Rondo Publications

Kevin Crossley-Holland   **At Mycenae**

The marble still bleeds, Clytemnestra.
Blame Homer.
If only historians and epic poets
Would also record the unspectacular.
Sheep bleat amongst the shrub
On the hillside opposite.
The lives of shepherds
Were not affected seriously at the time,
And time barely touches them.
Now the sheep move on their runs
And a light wind carries
To the stillness of the palace
A sweet wash once more
Of distant, ordinary bells.

The Dream-House Deutsch

Kevin Crossley-Holland   **Apologia**

You thought it was not good enough
to write finely-wrought verses
about archaeological remains
and cited Brecht: *What times are these*
when it is almost a crime to talk
about trees because it implies
silence about so many atrocities?
You are passionate but humourless.
Not all poets need or even should
redeem the squalid deals
of politicians by pleading
common causes, rights, denominators.
There are such world wonders: even today

regular, irregular flint-grey waves
under the tower, the first lamb there
amongst stones and discoloured bones.
There are so many languages
for our recurring crises,
and many great poems penned by men
who didn't give a damn for politics.
You are so arrogant.
What leads you to suppose
we can do with less of such hopeful diversity,
or even that we have different intentions?

The Dream-House Deutsch

A plain girl moving simply enough
Until love turned her down flat,
Leaving her with her parents' lives to live
And trunk full of embroidered stuff.

She acknowledged her plainness thereafter,
Underlined it rigorously
With all the farm work she could find.
Forgot the knack of easy laughter.

Her sisters watched how her coarseness grew,
Saw time-killing work broaden her hands
And gait, watched her gather a man's strength
To herself in the only way that she knew.

Guardedly her brothers watched her come and go,
Kept an eye on her many distances
As though she were the unpredictable horse
They enclosed in the furthest meadow.

Her meagre words the family understood
And they never forget to turn away
When, with a quiet ferocity,
She chopped unnecessary piles of wood.

A Stranger Here Secker & Warburg

The poets who never grow old —
They are one of our many loves.
It is as if their drownings,
Their suicides and interminable coughing
Are just so much more poetry
Completing something unfinished in ourselves.

How long it takes —
The cultivation of formal laurels —
And when we come across a photograph
Of an enlarged poet prospering in a warm climate,
Unrecognisable in a hat and whiskers,
What inescapable prose confronts us.

A Stranger Here Secker & Warburg

Jim Howell   **The Tarn**

No place as lonely; there was nothing
there but the water and a wind
herding the grass, and stones
sharp and hostile. I had seen
the place on the map, a blue spot
lost in the contours. Nothing to hint
of this, just the hills marked clear
as if it were theirs to compel
only — a landmark, a draughtsman's blot.

The sea is huge but here was anger
and silence. I came down the slope
to the tarn, for my first time
knowing water. Who drowned
here would drown hard, the lungs
ice-packed. Grass moved
from the edge; stones, black and dry

bit the feet. It had gathered hills
for its stillness and laid them
rugged and humble, as borders. Rain
it had hoarded and hardened. Glass
in the wind; I left it, afraid
of its threat and smallness. Over
the next rise and the next I took it.

Survivals Harry Chambers/Peterloo Poets

Jim Howell   **Evening Blackbird**

The clouds hang upside down and black;
chimneys are threatened and the mad wind bangs

its fist round corners. Through it all,
arms by his side, tail cocked for dusk,
the blackbird answers back.

The answer is a song — no malice there,
just incorruptibility, a sound
like a full stop to doubt or what
burdens the heart with words, a call
as innocent as air.

I stand and revel in the sight
of pure commitment, feeling that it comes
from somewhere long ago, this great
sensitive, elemental, calm
argument with the night.

Survivals Harry Chambers/Peterloo Poets

Jim Howell   **Hereford**
for my father

'It was beautiful', you said, not wishing then
I knew to intrude too much or to give
the words consciousness or perhaps the power
to hurt or be denied. 'It was beautiful', simply.

'The fields were all golden', you said of a pilgrimage
on a work's day trip where you slipped your frame
of brick for a sudden hunger of trees and harvest's
astonishing rust. 'All golden', is what you said.

Now as I drive from Wales through the same landscape,
from thirty years ago your words burn again;
your face comes easily, reminding me
of all you felt and how I could never answer.

So this is for Hereford where you came
only once, but loving the place took it
away with you like a locket to remember
always, to grow familiar and your own;

and for you, because you make me see
these fields with your eyes, feeling your mark
on them for ever, made special now and changed
by your once only coming.

Survivals Harry Chambers/Peterloo Poets

Documents, scrutinies, barriers,
Everywhere I pass through them,
It seems, without difficulty.
Nothing jars, nothing slips out of place,
Authority is satisfied by my credentials.

Really, it must represent some peak
Of achievement, from a Jewish
Point of view, that is.
                    What a time
It's taken to bring me
To this sort of freedom,
What tolls have been paid
To let me come
                    to this kind
Of passage.

I can appreciate it,
                    believe me,
I can appreciate.
But I find myself wondering,
As I sit at this café table

                    over

A good glass of beer,
Why I don't feel something more
                              like gratitude,
Why there's some form of acceptance
I don't grasp.

The Proper Blessing The Menard Press

A.C. Jacobs   **Mr Markson**

That old man who came to teach me then
Has blended with many.
                          I can hardly remember now
Just what he looked like,
                          except his black hat,
Yellowish stained beard, and shoulders hunched.
His accent too evades me
                          except that it was broken
Like my grandmother's.

A dark, grey, distant, forgettable man,
Yet three times a week at the dining-room table
He would point to the curling Hebrew script
and pour into me all it said about Creation,
The fall of Adam, and the faith of Abraham.

There was a piety,
                          and something more I couldn't
Understand in all that legend and recital:
A yearning in the old man's broken voice.

The Proper Blessing The Menard Press

A.C. Jacobs   **Where**

I find it is Yom Kippur,
                          and here I am
Down by the river
                          in late afternoon.
There is a poem
                          I have read

56

In several versions
                    about the Jewish writer
Who doesn't fast, who
                    doesn't go to synagogue
On Yom Kippur,
                    the day of atonement,
And here is my construction
                    of that poem.

Here am I,
                    on the embankment
Staring at the river,
                    while the lights
Are coming up,
                    signifying darkness, the end of the fast,
Though it's not over yet,
                    and the congregations
Are still gathered
                    in the synagogues,
Praying, *slach lonu, m'chal lonu,*
                    forgive us, pardon us,
We have sinned,
                    we deserve punishment,
We are like clay
                    in the hands of the great Potter,
Who has shaped us all,
                    even, you could say, me
Here by the river,
                    watching the water
And the rubbish
                    drifting on the water,
Imagining what is
                    swaying in under the bridges,
Is something of exile,
                    formless but perceptible,
Bringing in the names
                    of pious cities,
Vilna and Minsk and Vitebsk
                    (my own ancestral names)

And vanished communities,
                              behind curtains
Of forgetfulness,
                    and ordinary human change,
Praying communities
                    on Yom Kippur and other days
Clinging to and turning from
                              that which I cling to
And turn from,
                    if you like, the covenant
That keeps me fasting,
                         but not in synagogue
To-day, Yom Kippur.
                    I go into the gardens,
Sit down on a bench,
                    read my newspaper
And wait
          for the first star.

The Proper Blessing The Menard Press

As if the ultramarine of crest, breast,
Neck and the cry of "rape!" were not enough
    To startle one,
The peacock hoists an emperor's parasol
Inset with irridescent paste, fringed
    With flakes of sun,
Sparks, flames . . . Treading the moist lawn
He nods absurdly with each weighty step:
    Impossible —
Were it not for the evidence of a hundred eyes!
I can't believe he's fitter to survive
    Than a bushfull
Of sparrows and other plain fry; he looks
More like a last fling before the extinction
    Of all such tricks;
Like dinosaurs that took their cue from mountains
Before they fell, famished, into the sand;
    Like the phoenix
Which threw restraint to the four winds and caught
Fire from its own temper, feathers fanned
    To white heat;
Like man who outreaches death, but knowing the end
Is near, makes preparation for that departure
    His gaudiest feat.

Poetry and Paradox The Keepsake Press

Alasdair Maclean   **The Trees**

On the slope above a house where I once stayed
were trees, thick miles of them, not oaks, not tame,
no English wood but dark trees of the north,
an army poised until its signal came,

forever poised or for a day or two,
till birds flew past the houses's silly door
and nested where they pleased and cobwebs hung
like tapestries and mosses hushed the floor.

Then they would move out, seedlings, roots, downhill,
not knowing, caring, how the years should pass.
O that would be a brave pathetic sight,
high trees slow stepping down through the long grass!

Meanwhile the trees kept guard and kept the hill
but kept no least remembrance of the sky.
Few came about that area by choice
and none but carried fire as he went by.

Within those bounds, I knew, would fall enough
of weight on me to force me to my knees.
A hundred yards beyond the fence I still
could feel the downward pressure of the trees.

I was a child again and could not stay
away but watched and watched for all my care
and when I called my fearful question out
I heard the old appalling answer there.

A stone lobbed in proved nothing nor disproved,
not near nor far nor early thrown nor late.
It seems the forest was a desert too
and knew no life save what was corporate.

One boy before me left his books and games
and left undrunk whatever filled his cup
and walked into those trees and was not found.
Who sinks in that embrace is not cast up!

If there were times for tales, if there were time!
I'll not renounce the world and the world's goods.
But wait, old sweetheart, wait till Judgement Day
when all the babes come home to all the woods.

The lovely melancholy of the trees!
Horror Sylvanum some ancient called that ill
who lived in a great forest of the north
and could not leave it of his own free will.

Waking the Dead Gollancz

Alasdair Maclean   **Question and Answer**

'Do you love me? Do you love me?'
Your voice goes on and on
like a trailhound giving tongue.
'Say you love me then. I want to hear you say it.'
I say that once, when I was very young,
I saw a rat caught in a trap,
in a wire cage, squealing and snapping.
The cage was lowered into a tank of water.
I watched the stream of bubbles ease off
and at long last stop
and when the cage was hoisted to the top
the dead rat dangled from the roof,
its jaws so firmly clenched around the wire
they had to be levered free.

But I say all this to myself;
to you I mutter, sullenly but truthfully,
the words you want to hear.
Made easy then, you turn your back for sleep
and I lie where my love has left me,
a half-formed sadness in my bones
that will not waste or keep
and all around the water filling,
rising year by year,
and getting darker still above me,
getting dark and very deep.

Waking the Dead Gollancz

Katharine Middleton   **Drama Notice – Delayed**

After the long, tedious train journey north –
cabs trotting through the usual Sunday rain
from railway station to Theatre Royal.
Dress-baskets opened, digs found, the company
stands down till Monday morning rehearsal.

Now, stage-manager and leading man
stroll out along side streets for a breath of air.
Singing from some tin tabernacle draws them in
for shelter from a downpour, for a laugh, or both.
If the jeune premier came to scoff, he remain'd to pray.

Entreaties, arguments, avail them nothing. Converted,
he's seen the light that will darken all his days.
He'll never set foot on a stage again, or play
the part he was born for. The engagement ends.
He and his wife and child remain behind.

So the foresworn Hamlet fritters his life away –
clerk, office-cleaner, watchman – anything. Locks up
playbills, press-cuttings. Lives more than half
on his wife's courage and work. Assiduous at The Room,
searches Scripture in the slough of religious despond.

His understudy forges ahead to fame and knighthood.
Says, years after, over an *Ivy* lunch: 'He threw away
more than I ever had!' But to a child, known only
in leaf-thin, gentle, Bible-tormented old age,
a half-feared ghost.

Yet, grandfather, each year since your death
your stature's grown. Intransigent, at any cost
to self and others, for a creed I've no use for –
you stood firm. Loving you now, I applaud
your greatest role, played to an empty house.

Water Lane The Mandeville Press

Katharine Middleton   **Her Death**

Her death, and the soot-blackened hospital wall
ten minutes behind him,
he comes down the deserted road
to the bus-stop where no one's waiting.

The concrete shelter is roofed and open-fronted;
shaped, he's thought often these last few weeks,
like a pavilion for spectators
at a tournament, at games.

Now it flies great flags — night's navy-blue,
white pennons of the bleak street-lights,
and the colourless, all-coloured
flags of chaos.

At the edge of the world
he stands looking out on the mists of space.
Out there the arena, the tiers of seats,
lie empty.

The bus from Andromeda arrives.
The return-half of his ticket will take him
somewhere, even though the place he set out from
will no longer be there.

Water Lane The Mandeville Press

Ewart Milne **When You Were Sick and Ill**

When you were sick and ill
I often urged in being helpful
   Get better, love, quickly get better
And shortly in some amazing way you would
So fast I'd boast it was due to me you did
But I knew in fact it was just you and nature

I hope someday it doesn't happen
I'll say it when you will not listen
Or cannot rather as you slowly deafen
Until you lie stretched cold and still
As long ago had lain my mother
When inch by inch she died and I died with her

I wouldn't want to die much more than then
And call myself alive or ever move again
With any luck the cards will fall the other way
And you will say *Get better, love* to no reply
It seldom happens friends or lovers die together
Go down the road where all the signs point Nowhere

Or where you will:Heaven Hell Oblivion or to the Sea:
Though we two might prefer to go twined lovingly
But it shouldn't matter
Our covenant's with life as well as with each other
And we've no covenant with death at all:
Front-runners run although their team-mates flag and fall

Cantata Under Orion Aquila

Elma Mitchell   **Thoughts After Ruskin**

Women reminded him of lilies and roses.
Me they remind rather of blood and soap,
Armed with a warm rag, assaulting noses,
Ears, neck, mouth and all the secret places:

Armed with a sharp knife, cutting up liver,
Holding hearts to bleed under a running tap,
Gutting and stuffing, pickling and preserving,
Scalding, blanching, broiling, pulverising,
—All the terrible chemistry of their kitchens.

Their distant husbands lean across mahogany
And delicately manipulate the market,
While safe at home, the tender and the gentle
Are killing tiny mice, dead snap by the neck,
Asphyxiating flies, evicting spiders,
Scrubbing, scouring aloud, disturbing cupboards,
Committing things to dustbins, twisting, wringing,
Wrists red and knuckles white and fingers puckered,
Pulpy, tepid. Steering screaming cleaners
Around the snags of furniture, they straighten
And haul out sheets from under the incontinent
And heavy old, stoop to importunate young,
Tugging, folding, tucking, zipping, buttoning,
Spooning in food, encouraging excretion,
Mopping up vomit, stabbing cloth with needles,
Contorting wool around their knitting needles,
Creating snug and comfy on their needles.

Their huge hands! their everywhere eyes! their voices
Raised to convey across the hullabaloo,
Their massive thighs and breasts dispensing comfort,
Their bloody passages and hairy crannies,
Their wombs that pocket a man upside down!

And when all's over, off with overalls,
Quickly consulting clocks, they go upstairs,
Sit and sigh a little, brushing hair,
And somehow find, in mirrors, colours, odours,
Their essences of lilies and of roses.

The Poor Man in the Flesh
Harry Chambers/Peterloo Poets

"Art" she wrote "is a house
Which tries to be haunted"
Always the same choice —
Wake the dead
Or pack up and go.
Art is Yes or No.

Even after a lifetime
To move out, admit
"The place was fine,
I liked it
But who came there?"
Staying is nowhere.

Yet all of us stay
Or, at least, most.
Who dares say
He has seen no ghost
And never will?
Truth can kill.

Safer, by far, to wait
In a pleasant room,
Plan, decorate —
It must happen soon.
Get off to a good start.
Patience is an art.

Our Ship Secker & Warburg

F. Pratt Green   **The Old Couple**

The old couple in the brand-new bungalow,
Drugged with the milk of municipal kindness,
Fumble their way to bed. Oldness at odds
With newness, they nag each other to show
Nothing is altered, despite the strangeness
Of being divorced in sleep by twin-beds,
Side by side like the Departed, above them
The grass-green of candlewick bedspreads.

In a dead neighbourhood, where it is rare
For hooligans to shout or dogs to bark,
A footfall in the quiet air is crisper
Than home-made bread; and the budgerigar
Bats an eyelid, as sensitive to disturbance
As a distant needle is to an earthquake
In the Great Deep, then balances in sleep.
It is silence keeps the old couple awake.

Too old for loving now, but not for love,
The old couple lie, several feet apart,
Their chesty breathing like a muted duet
On wind instruments, trying to think of
Things to hang on to, such as the tinkle
That a budgerigar makes when it shifts
Its feather weight from one leg to another,
The way, on windy nights, linoleum lifts.

The Old Couple Harry Chambers/Peterloo Poets

I put my book on the table,
stretch myself.
I am tired.
The time has come again
for wandering around the room
before I am allowed to go to bed.
I switch the record-player off,
pull out the plug
and push the point-switch up.
Then I tidy my desk
and I tidy it again,
again,
and just before I leave the room
I wander over
to the record-player
and check the point again.
I switch off the light,
and leave the room,
and close the door.
And open the door again,
make sure the light's out,
peer beneath the shade
and eye the bulb.
I go back to the door,
switch on the light,
so that I know for sure what's on,
what's off,
then turn out the light again.
And leave the room,
and close the door.
And open the door again.
Admit the fucking light is off,
suppose it's safe
to go to bed at last.

The Same River Twice Carcanet

David Wright   **Procession**

Sober the overhead trees, and fields tilted
And framed by laborious walls on the framing hills,
No colour but a heavy green of August
Till the sun steps over a cloud, and light falls bare
On a pastoral lake and valley, where tourists
In their bright anoraks have come to stare.

Beyond the rectory, over the stone bridge,
The band assembles, cardigans and gleaming brass,
Waits by the teashop and nursery gardens;
A trombone has gone to the gents in the coach park.
Under the church tower, among those gaily
Shirted, I take my place, a sight-seer.

From its due angle the afternoon sunlight
Glances on us, the children in white and green,
The boys with rushes and the girls garlanded,
And on the gravemounds lies, autumnal almost.
The parishioners, in Sunday best, are ready
To move in procession. The Rush-bearing at Grasmere

Begins to parade toward the Rothay Hotel
Slowly; band, vicar, sidesmen, and choir,
With hesitant banners, the living, and the new-born
In perambulators gaudy with flowers.
Out of sight now, turning the corner, they'll return
A moment later, as they did last year.

What hymn is the band playing? They reappear,
The local dwellers followed by children,
Here and now, past and to be contained together;
Like the plain water that stumbles below
The bridge I stand on, keeping the bed of the stream,
So altering that it seems never to alter.

A View of the North Carcanet

71

Poets in Focus

The last notice of C. Day Lewis's verse to appear in the *Times Literary Supplement* was a review of *The Whispering Roots* in 1970. At that time, Day Lewis was Poet Laureate, and *TLS* reviewers were still anonymous. It is one of the few instances I can recall when I regretted the custom of anonymity, for the reviewer had taken the occasion to launch a general assault against his subject, in terms that seemed to me crude and vicious. The poet, he said, was all masks and no reality; his poems were mere acts of the will; they were frigid, wordy, and vulgar, and somehow threatened the good health of literature. There were, apparently, no exceptions, not one good word to be said about even a single poem. It was not so much a review, I thought, as a literary mugging.

Now that Day is no longer a living laureate, but simply a dead poet, perhaps the time has come to consider his work more temperately, to forgive him the great gifts that he did not have (and never claimed), and to value what he had, and what he achieved. To do that we might best begin at the end, in the Stinsford churchyard where he is buried not far from the grave of Thomas Hardy. His burial there seems to me entirely appropriate, not because he was of the stature of Hardy, who seems more and more clearly to be the greatest of modern English poets, but because he was of Hardy's company, a decent minor poet in the same tradition.

If even Day Lewis's most friendly critics have not always seen him clearly in that tradition, they have had reasons for confusion. For one thing, he found his poetic place relatively late, after much searching and much imitating, and his earlier books are full of echoes of other poets, so much so that they often seem to have no more unity of style than an anthology of modern verse has. From his earliest contributions to *Oxford Poetry* to the last poem in *Whispering Roots* he found it easier to speak in other voices than in his own: first the early Yeats and then the later, then Auden — all those kestrels and airmen — and after that Edward Thomas, Eliot, de la Mare, Frost, Hardy.

Day Lewis was quite aware that he was an imitative poet, though he sometimes tried to find a less pejorative way oɪ putting it. In 1951, in a preface to the Penguin Poets selection of his verse, he wrote of his kind of poet:

If, like myself, he is a writer still much open to the influence of other poets, he will often find that he has more or less consciously used some other poet to mediate between his material and his imagination. I myself have been technically influenced, and enabled to clarify my thoughts, by such diverse poets as Yeats, Wordsworth, Robert Frost, Virgil, Valéry, W. H. Auden, and Hardy. They suggested to me ways of saying what I had to say.

Sixteen years later, in another introduction, he offered another list:

It is easy to see the influences: Yeats, for example, the English Metaphysicals, Hopkins, Auden, Hardy, Meredith, Frost. Mediators, I would prefer to call them, rather than influences; for they are men whose work helped me to approach and open up new fields for my own verse, made me aware of the potentiality in subjects I had previously ignored, and showed me a way in to them. Such was the benign effect of these poets. If an influence proved bad for me in the longer run, it was through my over-susceptibility to other men's way of using words, so that I found myself imitating instead of deriving.

If these self-explanations seems unconvincing to a modern reader, that may be partly the reader's fault, or modernism's fault. For what Day Lewis was arguing was essentially the classical defence of imitation; and in a time like our own, when influence is regarded as an anxiety rather than as a customary support for the imagination, such a traditional attitude is bound to be puzzling.

The other principal obstacle to a just assessment of his achievement is, of course, his connection with the other principal poets of his generation. The swift emergence of a new generation of poets in the early 1930s blurred the differences among them, and did some damage to the individual reputations of all the poets concerned. "How odd it is," Auden wrote in the 1960s,

to recall that at one time there stalked through the pages of literary journalism a curious chimera named *Daylewisaudenmacneicespender.* To be sure, four poets of more or less the same age, from more or less the same social background, confronted by the same historical events, will exhibit certain responses in common, but it should have been obvious that what we happened to have in common was the least interesting thing about us, that whatever there may be of value in what we have written is peculiar to each of us.

Perhaps it should have been obvious, but it wasn't. And it was made less obvious by the efforts of all the others, on occasion, to write as though they were Auden. But the four of them were not a school; they were simply four poets, of whom the most gifted and most aggressive dominated the others. All of them (even Auden) cast off the early Auden influence eventually, but Day Lewis, because he had the slightest individual gift, and was the least sure of his own poetic identity, was the most influenced, and the last to break free.

For him, and I think also for most of his generation, the coming of the Second World War was a profoundly liberating experience. The decade of the 1930s had been a time when political action seemed urgent and unavoidable, and every poem was a political act. Day Lewis entered that political world more completely and more naively than most of his contemporaries, and wrote some very embarrassing verse (the sonnet beginning "Yes, why do we all, seeing a Red, feel small?" must be one of the worst political poems ever written). In later years he was inclined to minimise this part of his early work: "During my so-called political period", he wrote in the 1950s, "most of my poems were in fact above love and death." In a sense this is true, but the point is that in the 1930s all private experience and feelings, even love and death, were touched by public issues. A fair example is Day Lewis's own sequence of poems, *From Feathers to Iron* (1931): "For me," he wrote, the sequence "expressed simply my thoughts and feelings during the nine months before the birth of my first child," but "the critics, almost to a man, took it for a political allegory." To a degree the critics were right; the sequence does contain politics, because everything did then.

The war changed all that, and made it possible for Day Lewis to be what he had always been at heart — a private, lyric poet. Perhaps the simplest way to describe the nature of that transformation is to say that the coming of war changed the poet's relation to time. To be political is to be concerned with the present and the future, with, one might say, public time. But in a war the present is beyond any man's control, and the future does not exist. And so the poet was freed to turn backward, to the past, the time in which we live our most private lives. "During the last war," he later wrote, "I found myself able to use in verse for the first time images out of my own childhood." He stopped talking about poetry and propaganda and the poet's role, and began to define poetry in terms of the recovered past: "Every poem is an attempt to compose our memories," he wrote; and "the poet's prime motive is a felt compulsion, a duty to discover himself through his memories." As a source for the materials of poetry, the private past had replaced the public present.

Most of Day Lewis's best poems were written during this period of wartime liberation and just after. This was also the time when the many influences on his poetry became mainly one. Those apparently random lists that he made of poets he had learned from obscure one important point, that in his imitating he had gradually moved toward certain poets who resemble each other, and who belong to the native English tradition to which his own nature and talents were best suited. We may for convenience's sake call it the Hardy tradition, since Hardy has been its principal transmitter to the twentieth century, but it obviously has a history that is older than Hardy, that includes, for instance, Wordsworth and Clare, and has its roots in medieval lyrics.

It is a tradition with many variations, but its constants seem to me to be these: it is English, and is primarily concerned with actual nature in the English countryside, and with man's relation to it; it is physical not transcendental; it is descriptive not symbolic; it is retrospective, often regretful and melancholy, but also ironic and stoic. Formally, the tradition is conservative but inventive: Hardy played endless variations on inherited stanza forms, and rarely repeated one, and Day Lewis was the same sort of craftsman. In *Whispering Roots,* for example, there are thirty-seven different stanzas in thirty-four poems, and only one is repeated.

The Hardy tradition has lived quietly on through many changes of literary fashion; it survived the Pound era (without really even noticing it), and it will surely go on surviving as long as English poets find it possible to think of themselves as English. The line after Hardy is clear enough if you stop to think about it: Edward Thomas, the early, rhyming Lawrence, Graves, Blunden, de la Mare, Andrew Young,

Grigson, Larkin. Not all of them have attracted the attention of the weighty modernist critics and anthologists (though Larkin's *Oxford Book* gives the tradition generous attention); but they are surely more often read voluntarily, outside classrooms, by people who simply enjoy reading poetry, than most of the major modernists are.

Day Lewis is clearly in this tradition, and it was when he had found his place there in the neighbourhood of Hardy that he could begin to write his best verse. That he had freed himself from other influences only to assume a single and more powerful one is not to his discredit: it is characteristic, and indeed definitive of good minor poets that they depend on major ones. If they are fortunate, they find a stronger voice that is enough like their own to permit them to speak through it in their own accents. When such a poet finds the right tradition, his voice will sound true, not because it is his but because it is the tradition's: when he chooses unwisely, he will simply sound like a bad imitator. Day Lewis's efforts to write like Auden fail both as imitations and as poems; but his poems in the Hardy tradition succeed, and though they remind us of Hardy, they retain their own individuality, they are not imitations but new poems.

An example of what I mean is "Cornet Solo", one of the first of Day Lewis's Hardyesque poems. It begins:

> *Thirty years ago lying awake,*
> *Lying awake*
> *In London at night when childhood barred me*
> *From livelier pastimes, I'd hear a street-band break*
> *Into old favourites – "The Ash Grove",*
>
>   *"Killarney"*
> *Or "Angels Guard Thee".*
>
> *That was the music for such an hour –*
> *A deciduous hour*
> *Of leaf-wan drizzle, of solitude*
> *And gaslight bronzing the gloom like an autumn*
>   *flower –*
> *The time and music for a boy imbrued*
> *With the pensive mood.*

Everything here — the situation itself, the repetitions, the diction, the pensive mood — reminds one of Hardy. Yet the poem is more than imitative; it has Day Lewis's own mark upon it. Its tone is softer, its irony less relentless, its movement less crabbed than a Hardy version would be; it belongs, not to Hardy, but to the tradition.

By the time his next volume, *Poems 1943-1947,* was written, Day Lewis was easy enough with his place in the tradition to celebrate some of its members by name: there are poems addressed to Hardy, to Blunden, and to de la Mare. There are also many fluent poems in the traditional manner, poems that show his confidence in his ability to use it: "A Failure", "The Unwanted", "Statuette: Late Minoan". Like *Word Over All,* the book has a unity of tone that none of the earlier collections had.

After the poems of the 1940s the Hardy tradition is less clear in Day Lewis's poems, though it never fades out entirely. In the later poems, irony melts into nostalgia, the past overshadows the natural present, and the tone becomes quietly reflective and meditative. A major poet like Hardy could go on in the manner that suited him, becoming more and more like himself, but in Day Lewis's later work one feels a kind of easing of poetic tension, a relaxing into retrospection. A paradigmatic poem for this state is one in which the aging poet looks at an old photograph and recalls past emotions. There are several such poems among the later work: "The Album", "Father to Sons", "The House Where I Was Born" — all depending on the instant nostalgia that old photographs create (and not, as would be the case with Hardy, on the present intensity of past feelings). Another characteristic occasion (one that Hardy also exploited in poems of his old age) is the return to scenes of childhood; all the poems in the first part of *The Whispering Roots,* his last book, are about Ireland, where he was born. They are not exactly the poems of a revenant: Day Lewis was only two when he left Ireland, and he returned, as he says in a poem, with "no drowned memories". They are, rather, the poems of an elderly man in search of a past, one more step in that search for identity that had led him through other men's styles and other men's subjects, and finally back into himself.

Other late poems are records of ordinary occasions — moving house, recovering from an illness, seeing a merry-go-round or a snowfall — each moulded into a single metaphor, of vision or of loss. This kind of poetry, the habitual casting of common-place things into verse, becomes inevitably a kind of autobiography, told with reticence (that too is in the tradition), but none the less an essentially personal record. Day Lewis's whole life is in his poems: childhood, adolescent love, marriage, the births of children, politics and the end of politics, the break-up of a marriage, later love, his own last illness. In cases like his, the life's work is really a single poem, and individual parts do not stand out from the whole. Perhaps that is why there is still no Day Lewis canon, and no single poem as well known as, say, Spender's "I think continually", or MacNeice's "Sunlight on the Garden". Day Lewis was simply not an anthology poet: but then, neither was Hardy.

Times Literary Supplement

Donald Davie is still thought of as a 'Movement' poet, that is, one who made his name in the 1950s, publishing his poems in the same places as other university-based poets such as John Wain and Kingsley Amis. You will find this matter of the 'Movement' well treated in John Press's *Map of Modern English Verse;* I mention it right at the start, because I am going to pay more attention to Davie's poetry of the sixties and seventies than to the earlier work, and I hope that you will, therefore, supplement my account with the material you will find in Press's very useful book.

Davie's first book of poems was paper-bound, slim and elegantly, though not expensively, printed by Oscar Mellor at his Fantasy Press outside Oxford; it was called *Brides of Reason,* and it appeared in 1955. His first book of literary criticism, *Purity of Diction in English Verse,* had been published three years earlier, cloth-bound by the firm of Chatto & Windus, the publishers also of F. R. Leavis, William Empson and other distinguished critics. The contrast tells something of the temper of the times, when literary criticism was far more saleable than new verse: indeed the reasoning quality of Davie's first poems, like those of fellow 'Movement' poets, was ascribed to the influence of critics like Empson and Leavis. There certainly was, and still is, cross-fertilisation between his work as critic and teacher of literature and his work as poet. *Purity of Diction,* which deals largely with English poetry of the eighteenth century, was written he has told us, 'principally so as to understand what I had been doing, or trying to do, in the poems I had been writing. Under a thin disguise the book was, as it still is, a manifesto (*Purity of Diction,* revised ed., 1967, p. 197).

If 'eighteenth century' suggests elegance and idle conventionality to you (of course, it should not), then it may not be immediately obvious what the writers of that time can have to do with such a view of poetry as this:

> *A poem is less an orange than a grid;*
> *It hoists a charge; it does not ooze a juice.*
> *It has no rind, being entirely hard.*

('Poem as abstract', *Brides of Reason*)

Surely *this* is a modern poem, one might say, pointing to the aggressive diction of 'hoist a charge' or the pseudo-rhyme of 'grid' and 'hard'. Yet it has its base in the poetic practice of the eighteenth century after all, not merely because it is a poetry of statement. Its hardness is merely a twentieth-century version of Augustan 'strength'. This is something that Davie discusses in *Purity of Diction,* the focal point being Dr. Johnson's commentary on the not-quite-eighteenth-century poet, Sir John Denham (1615-1669), in his *Lives of the Poets.* According to Johnson, 'strength' in Denham 'is to be found in many lines and couplets, which convey much meaning in few words, and exhibit the sentiment with more weight than bulk'. It is Davie's aim in many of the poems of *Brides of Reason* to achieve 'strength' of this kind.

You might take a look at the poem 'On Bertrand Russell's "Portraits from Memory",' which John Press reprints in his *Map,* for an example of this weightily concise style at its best; consider the second line of its last stanza:

> *It was the Muse that could not make her home*
> *In that too thin and yet too sluggish air . . .*

That is the Davie of the fifties, and the virtues of elegant, assured, rational wit displayed in John Press's other choice, 'The Fountain', (from the 1957 volume *A Winter Talent*) may be seen to arise naturally from the 'strength' of the earlier poems, and to be admirable. In the second book, indeed, the tendency to obscurity of utterance, which may derive from Empson's influence, has disappeared, what ambiguousness there may be in the style working now only to the poetry's advantage.

The significant changes in Davie's work do not appear, however, until *after* the publication of *A Winter Talent.* Press quotes from an essay Davie wrote in 1959 called 'Remembering the Movement' (*Map,* p. 260) in which he passes judgement on his own work and that of his fellow 'Movement' poets:

> Hardly ever did we seem to write our poems out of an idea of
> poetry as a way of knowing the world we were in, apprehending
> it, learning it; instead we conceived of it as an act of private and

public therapy, the poet resolving his conflicts by expressing them and proffering them to the reader so that vicariously he should do the same.

The later poetry, from *The Forests of Lithuania* (1959) on, may be seen as aiming at a way of knowing the world we are in, as turned away from the extreme self-consciousness of the 'Movement' in favour of commitment to the world beyond the self, absorption in experience of the world shared with others. Davie's 'strength' here serves different purposes.

Naturally, given the change of direction in his poetry towards the world of other people's experience, Davie's place in that world matters. In particular, it matters that, like many people in this century, Davie does not have one place that he can call his own. His life reflects the mobility of our phase of western civilisation. Fewer and fewer people still live in the place where they were born. We are all used to the idea of going to live where we can find work. Davie was born in Barnsley in 1922, but he didn't stay there. From Barnsley Grammar School he went to St. Catharine's College, Cambridge, and followed that by a spell in the Navy that included eighteen months in the north of Russia and six in India and Ceylon. After graduate studies in Cambridge again, he took a first job in Dublin, where he spent seven years, then he taught one year in Santa Barbara, California, and in 1958 returned to Cambridge as a Lecturer in English. But he only spent six years there, for in 1964 he went as Professor of Literature to the new University of Essex. Four years later still he left for Stanford, where he seems to have settled.

Such a career in the last century would have denoted restlessness in the extreme. Today we cannot be so sure. The move from place to place is part of our way of life; and it is an important part of it. It is not merely a means of distinguishing us from the Victorians or the Edwardians, as our dress might be; it is positively a condition of the uncertainty in which we find ourselves when we contemplate the relatively settled system of values, moral and other, handed down to us by our parents and grandparents. Historically, it is our fortune *not* to be settled, *not* to have a place of our own, and to live, as a consequence, with a much reduced sense of abiding values. Davie's tender, affectionate reminiscence, ' "Abbey-forde" ', is, then, about *us:*

Thirty years unremembered,
Monkey-faced black-bead-silken
Great-aunt I sat across from,
Gaping and apprehensive,
The thought of you suddenly fits.
Across great distances
Clement time brings in its
Amnesties, Aunt Em.

'Abbeyforde': the name
Deciphered stood for Ford
Abbey, in Somerset, There
Your brother's sweetheart Nell,
My grandmother, drew him to her,
Whom later he pitchforked North.
Such dissolutions, Em!
Such fatal distances!

'Keep still feast for ever . . .!'
A glow comes up off the page
In which I read of a paschal
Feast of the diaspora
In Italy, in a bad
Time for the Jews, and it is
As if in that tender and sad
Light your face were illumined.

('Los Angeles Poems (1968–9)' *Collected Poems* p. 222)

This is an unassuming poem. We are made privy to a moment of intimate communion between the poet and the dead, communion no less loving or intense for its being coloured by humour, or for its taking up into itself the kind of commonplace fancy that does so often lie behind English house-names. It makes no direct onslaught on us: as the poet reads of the diaspora and think of the wanderings of his immediate forebears, we are led merely by human sympathy to think of our own selves and our families. What binds us to the poem is our recognisably sharing a world with it; and what we value it for, if we read it rightly, is

85

the way it commemorates and embodies love as an active and commanding force, an abiding value, in that world. Perhaps, then, the poem is only unassuming because it is in the nature of the fundamental to be overlooked; what it commemorates is so much part of us that we don't notice it. The poem takes us back to the fundamental rock-nature of love, abiding as the memory in the house-name, abiding as the memory on which the poem itself is founded, and it would be less than truthful were it to seek to transform the quite ordinary love it celebrates.

In the way it appeals to a common experience, "Abbeyforde" is markedly different from even the minor poems of the masters of the first half of the century, Eliot and Yeats. They admonish, they exhort, they curse, they pray, but they rarely work in the modest fashion of Davie's poetry. The difference is not accidental; it is a difference of stance. Davie is among us, living with us; his predecessors were in important ways outside the society for which they wrote. They saw themselves as prophet or priest; his role is that of a man speaking of men, a man speaking to men. A passage from Davie's book on modern British poetry is relevant here:

> . . . prophetic poetry is necessarily an inferior poetry . . . The prophet is above being fair-minded − judiciousness he leaves to someone else. But the poet will absolve himself from none of the responsibilities of being human, he will leave none of those responsibilities to 'someone else'. And being human involves the responsibility of being judicious and fair-minded. In this way the poet supports the intellectual venture of humankind, taking his place along with (though *above,* yet along with) the scholar and the statesman and the learned divine. His poetry supports and nourishes and helps to shape *culture;* the prophet, however, is outside culture and (really) at war with it. The prophet exists on sufferance, he is on society's expense account, part of what society can sometimes afford. Not so the poet; he is what society cannot dispense with.
>
> (*Thomas Hardy and British Poetry,* 1973, pp. 150-1)

These are the words of a poet who conceives of his art highly, and whose modesty reflects neither the exhaustion of a tradition nor the timidity of an individual, but a deliberated choice of virtues in his poetry akin to judiciousness and fair-mindedness – the fair-mindedness that looks back at Aunt Em and understands at last, is plain to see. These are the virtues which a society is unable to do without and which it is a poet's duty to strengthen.

In Davie we have to do with a poet who has applied himself just as much as Eliot or Yeats ever did to the problems of modern society, one who has fashioned a style and found a subject-matter appropriate to that society in much their way. Only he has rejected their stance, their removal in spirit from their own society. (When Davie writes about Eliot and Yeats – and he has done so at length about the former – he tends to underplay the prophetic role in Eliot, and to overplay it in Yeats.) The poet in the modern tradition whom Davie finds most congenial is Ezra Pound, about whom he has written two books; perhaps the reason is that Pound's wanderings, from the United States to London, to Paris, to Italy and so on, gave him a perspective on life, an attentiveness to things in themselves and to the idiosyncracies of place and custom, and even a modesty, which are all lacking in his rivals but which must commend themselves to such a poet of man-on-the-move as Davie. And Pound, by the way, whatever is said of him by the half-informed or the ignorant, *was* modest, and his modesty is at the heart of his great long poem *The Cantos,* as well as the basis of his many short poems. The sensibility that produced the lines:

> *Pull down thy vanity, it is not man*
> *Made courage, or made order, or made grace*
> *(Canto LXXXI)*

was of a piece with that which produced the line (about his own poem)

> *I cannot make it cohere*

and which sought 'To confess wrong without losing rightness' *(Canto CXVI).* Pound's modesty, Pound's heightened sense of human mobility (the protagonist of *The Cantos* is, in one light, Ulysses, the supreme wanderer of the western world), Pound's restatements of the most ancient human values ('What thou lovest well remains . . .'), all these are qualities held in common with Davie.

Add one more: Pound's awareness of *voice* as the medium of poetry, and his consequent opposition to what he termed 'the rhythm of the metronome'. In Pound's poetry this led to the adoption of free verse, a refusal to be content with the current notions of the rhythms permissible in English verse. 'I believe,' he said, 'in an absolute rhythm, a rhythm, that is, in poetry which corresponds exactly to the emotion or shade of emotion to be expressed'. Such exactitude seemed to demand, often, the 'freedom' of free verse.

Davie uses free verse — unrhymed, with no regular distribution of stress, with no established length of line — occasionally. He does not appeal to Pound's practice consistently, except in so far as it embodies Pound's principle: 'to compose in the sequence of the musical phrase, not in sequence of a metronome'. Sticking to that principle means attending very carefully to the potentialities of the human instrument, the voice. Davie has been helped in this not only by the example of Pound, but also by that of the Russian poet Boris Pasternak, who far excels Pound in richness of sound and rhythm.

His work has been of the greatest importance for Davie. Pasternak's *Poems 1955-59,* published with a good translation into English by Michael Harari (1960), radically changed the nature of Davie's poetry, revealing gifts hitherto unsuspected, allowing Davie to speak in his own voice by one of those fruitful exchanges between one culture and another of which Eliot's transmutation of French models gives us another example. *Events and Wisdoms* (1964) is the book in which this influence is first felt; it is also, and not by accident, that in which the idea of poetry as a way of knowing the world we are in finds its most complete expression.

It is embarrassing to have to insist upon the significance of so great a writer as Pasternak. Davie's interest in him has been a continuing one, manifest not only in imitations, adaptations and translations, but also in the commentary on *The Poems of Dr. Zhivago* (1963) and the selection of critical essays on the poet, made in collaboration with Angela Livingstone, and published in 1969 as *Pasternak.* He is a great man by virtue of his life as well as of his art. It is not going too far to describe that life in terms of moral heroism, a heroism in which devotion to his art and defence of the humane principles it embodies played a considerable part. Pasternak's seriousness, his sensuousness, his humour, his joy in life, religious in its depth, his love for all that was of its nature modest ('I do not believe in anything very big in size or in anything of which there is very much. Women give birth to people and not to cyclopses' (letter to N. G. Vachnadze, 31 December 1949, *Letters to Georgian Friends*, Penguin Books, 1971, p. 116)) — the combination of these qualities could not but impress Davie and have upon him a liberating effect.

Davie has always favoured traditional poetic forms. Rhyme and metre are important to him. Pasternak too uses such forms, but with a personal force that is lacking in many of his contemporaries. In this respect also he impressed Davie. It is worth contrasting such a poem as 'Limited Achievement' (from Davie's second book of poems, *A Winter Talent*), which demonstrates and yet protests against his own formal assurance as well as that of its ostensible subject, the engraver Piranesi, with a post-Pasternak poem, 'Vying', a poem bound together by modulations of the human voice in a manner close to that described by an early Russian critic of Pasternak: 'The lines are all fastened to one another by knots of intonation which carry the voice without pause for breath from one line to the next' (Nikolai Aseev, 'Melody or Intonation', *Pasternak*, ed. D. Davie and A. Livingstone 1969, p. 82). Speaking the poem lifts it off the page, and reveals its full meaning, as the words of a person in whose place the poem invites you, and to some extent obliges you, to stand. Just as in ' "Abbeyforde",' so in 'Vying', the poem rests on a necessary sense of the human voice:

> *Vying is our trouble;*
> *And a devious vice it is*
> *When we vie in abnegations,*
> *Services, sacrifices.*
>
> *Not to be devious now*
> *(For perhaps I would not begin*
> *Taking the blame for winning*
> *If this were not how to win),*
>
> *I assert that such is the case:*
> *I seem to have more resources;*
> *I thrive on enforcing the more*
> *The less naked the force is.*

Mutinies, sulks, reprisals,
All play into my hand;
To be injured and forgiving
Was one of the roles I planned.

Married to me, you take
The station I command,
As if in a peopled graveyard
Deserted in an upland.

There I, the sexton, battle
Earth that will overturn
Headstones, and rifle tombs,
And spill the tilted urn.

('Poems of 1962–3' *C.P.* p. 169)

I find it impossible to read this poem without hearing the natural inflexions of a man speaking, and I suggest that this naturalness is just what permits the poem to move into its surprising, beautiful ending, taking its logic not from what is said, but from what the necessary voice implies.

The attention to sound and rhythm, the variety of tone ('Mutinies, sulks, reprisals . . .'), the flexibility of a line not subdued to 'the rhythm of a metronome' – these are all qualities of the poetry of our own century deployed by Davie on behalf of a view of what our unsettled, our mobile society needs, the stability of judiciousness and fair-mindedness. It is our very rootlessness that makes such placeless, timeless little dramas as are the matter of 'Vying' important for us: our certainties have to be these, of personal pieties and honesties, and we would wish to possess them as completely as this poet, poised yet quick to each nuance of feeling, does here. Among his contemporaries Davie has one equal only in the evocation of such human assurances – Philip Larkin.

If though, we look to the past for a poetry similarly concerned for human values feelingly apprehended, and expressed, like Davie's, in a fashion that requires the human voice to complete the meaning of the verse, then we can find significant analogues for what Davie is attempting. Take a beautiful poem of his like 'Tunstall Forest'; originally printed in *Essex Poems* (1969):

90

> *Stillness! Down the dripping ride,*
> *The firebreak avenue*
> *Of Tunstall Forest, at the side*
> *Of which we sought for you,*
> *You did not come. The soft rain dropped,*
> *And quiet indeed we found:*
> *No cars but ours, and ours was stopped,*
> *Rainfall the only sound.*
> *And quiet is a lovely essence;*
> *Silence is of the tomb,*
> *Austere though happy; but the tense*
> *Stillness did not come,*
> *The deer did not, although they fed*
> *Perhaps nearby that day,*
> *The liquid eye and elegant head*
> *No more than a mile away*

(Essex Poems, *C.P.* p. 189)

Of course, this has to do once again with our mobility, not just superficially — 'No cars but ours' — but intrinsically: the quiet of the forest is valued *because* there were 'No cars but ours'. The more we do without rest and settledness — the more vividly we realise our own transience in our lives — the more we value rest and settledness when we come by them. In 'Tunstall Forest' we almost come by them — but not quite:

> *Stillness did not come,*
> *The deer did not, although they fed*
> *Perhaps nearby that day . . .*

Our mobility is contrasted with that of the deer: they *are* the stillness we lack. And, since this is the poem of a fair-minded poet, it is not all loss, that we lack their stillness. We can, at least, have quiet; and we can known that 'quiet' is not 'silence', just as it is not 'stillness'. Possessing these discriminations — and the poem reminds us that we do possess them, by making the voice complete their emphases ('*Silence* is of the tomb . . .') — we possess a world more various, as it were more responsive to our own various nature, than the deer can ever have.

The distinctions in this poem send us back to Davie's first book of literary criticism, *Purity of Diction in English Verse*. Johnson, illustrating the quality of 'strength', quotes among others, Denham's lines on Cowley:

> *To him no author was unknown,*
> *Yet what he wrote was all his own;*
> *Horace's wit and Virgil's state,*
> *He did not steal, but emulate!*
> *And when he would like them appear,*
> *Their garb, but not their clothes, did wear.*

Davie comments on these lines:

> It had not occurred to the reader that the distinction between 'garb' and 'clothes' was so fine and so definite. It is forced on his attention in a way that is salutary, pleasing, and relevant to the poet's theme.
>
> *(Purity of Diction in English Verse,* 1952, p. 65)

Just so is the distinction between 'stillness', 'quiet' and 'silence' forced on our attention in 'Tunstall Forest', and similarly needing to be completed by the emphasis of voice. (It is this emphasis *on* voice which, in my opinion, distinguishes Davie from another contemporary poet of 'strength', Geoffrey Hill, whose musicality is much closer to that of Eliot and Yeats than that of Pound, Pasternak and the eighteenth century.)

Davie's kind of 'strength' is associated with the use of a plain diction, drawing as much on the traditions of prose as on those of poetry. This too he derives from the eighteenth century, and it may be seen at work in 'Tunstall Forest', where it is a kind of leaven to the more poetical lines like 'But quiet is a lovely essence'. That is a poem of the sixties; Davie's first two books recall far more often, and it would seem intentionally, the formality, the accuracy, the prosaic strength of poets like Johnson, Goldsmith and Cowper. Take, for example, 'The Garden Party', which appeared in Davie's first book of poems, *Brides of Reason,* in 1955:

Above a stretch of still unravaged weald
In our Black Country, in a cedar-shade,
I found, shared out in tennis courts, a field
Where children of the local magnates played.

And I grew envious of their ease
In Scott Fitzgerald's unembarrassed vein.
Let prigs, I thought, fool others as they please,
I only wish I had my time again.

To crown a situation as contrived
As any in 'The Beautiful and Damned',
The phantom of my earliest love arrived;
I shook absurdly as I shook her hand.

As dusk drew in on cultivated cries,
Faces hung pearls upon a cedar-bough;
And gin could blur the glitter of her eyes,
But it's too late to learn to tango now.

My father, of a more submissive school,
Remarks the rich themselves are always sad.
There is that sort of equalizing rule;
But theirs is all the youth we might have had.
                                        (*C.P.* p. 15)

Here, the modern theme of the unsettled life is treated in a way quite different from that of those later poems which I have already quoted. ' "Abbeyforde" ' allows us to participate in the acts of the poet's memory in a way that is both intimate and quietly dramatic — dramatic enough to give the feeling of spontaneity to 'Such dissolutions, Em! Such fatal distances!' But participation is not exactly what 'The Garden Party' requires of us. The poet's hope, instead, is that we shall *concur* with what the poem says. It is a poem about distance — the distance between past and present, between father and son, between the youth that was ours and the one we wish had been ours. In sympathy with this, there is a distance between poet and reader, noticeable, for example, in the reticence of 'the phantom of my earliest love' (compare the 'monkey-faced' great-aunt) and only cancelled in the last line when at last the first person plural is used: 'theirs is all the youth *we* might have had.' At the poem's end we are to concur in a general statement about the rich, one which sums up and takes into itself, as it were, all the other distances of the poem. Such generalisation was congenial to Davie in his beginnings — 'my mind moves most easily and happily among abstractions, it relates ideas far more readily than it relates experience,' he noted of himself in those days. And his fondness for it was strengthened by his admiration for poets like Cowper or Goldsmith. To my mind, though, it is this poem's generalising mode that makes it, polished and elegant as it is, a minor thing. Such generalisation belongs to the eighteenth century; it is confident of values which are shared, of a community of feeling which in our time cannot be assumed, has to be won, as the obliquity of ' "Abbeyforde" ' or 'Tunstall Forest' does it.

> *Let observation with extensive view*
> *Survey mankind from China to Peru,*

said Johnson in *The Vanity of Human Wishes;* but for us the idea of such observation is daunting, the province of comparative studies even more specialised than the study of specific phenomena. We are only too conscious, perhaps, of the possibilities for individual bias in such general views to undertake them boldly in the spirit of Dr. Johnson. And indeed, the generalisation of 'The Garden Party' is limited by an individual bias too obvious in the poem, and we can only concur in its conclusion 'theirs is all the youth we had' in a kind of betrayal of whatever real joys the youth of those without 'moneyed ease' may bring. I am not suggesting, of course, that the poet did not feel this about his poem. Its plea for concurrence conceals a plea for something other than that, for human sympathy, and the poem depends on this fact for its pathos. But is is also limited by that. The openness to experience and to the reader which we find in the later poems is not to be found here: and yet such openness, such assurance of basic human qualities as are manifest, and with such wit and tenderness, in 'Vying', are the very qualities that our unsettledness requires.

Davie, then, is a poet who has changed and grown with the passing of time, yet without abandoning what was truly of value in his early work, its 'strength', the poetic use of a prosaic diction. The distinctions between words made in 'Tunstall Forest' are not of the same order as that contained in the line in 'The Garden Party' 'I shook absurdly as I shook her hand', but they are built upon that order. In 'Tunstall Forest' the poet's voice and stance are quite different. 'The Garden Party' does demand a certain kind of voice to complete its meaning: 'There is that sort of equalizing rule' — the tone is one of enforced reasonableness, a resigned detachment. But in 'Tunstall Forest', where the sentence uncoils at length, flexed against the regular alternation of line-strength we are close to a *developing* utterance, one whose responsive poise changes from one moment to another as perception itself shifts, sees further — we are, in short, close to those 'knots of intonation which carry the voice without pause from one line to the next' that Aseev admired in Pasternak. And to define the poet's stance in 'Tunstall Forest' we can also make reference to Pasternak:

> in his poems Pasternak is constantly fascinated by this capacity of poetry for renewing and refreshing perception — yet with this crucial difference, that for him it is poetry that does this, not the poet; that it is the world which thus renews itself, through the poet and his poem, but not at the poet's behest.
>
> (*Pasternak,* 1969, p. 19)

Is not perception so renewed (and 'not at the poet's behest') in 'Tunstall Forest'?

Pasternak's at any rate, was the example that brought to birth Davie's most memorable poems to date — *Events and Wisdoms* (1964) and *Essex Poems.* I don't want to emphasise the importance of Pasternak unduly, and it is true that Davie has shown *constant* change in his poetry — something which I am not able to illustrate fully here. But he himself has written about *the* change in his style, and has done so in a poem, 'Barnsley Cricket Club', which he has told us is derived, if remotely, from Pasternak. It originally appeared in *Events & Wisdoms.*

> *Now the heat comes, I am demoralized.*
> *Important letters lie unanswered, dry*
> *Shreds of tobacco spike the typewriter,*
> *No undertaking but is ill-advised.*

Unanswerable even the shortest missive,
Replies not sealed, or sealed without conviction.
Thumb-marks dry out, leaving the paper pouchy,
Tousled with effort, desperate, inconclusive.

'A thing worth doing is worth doing well,'
Says Shaw Lane Cricket Ground
Between the showers of a July evening,
As the catch is held and staid hand-clappings swell.

This almost vertical sun, this blaze of heat,
All stinging furze and snagged unravelling,
Denies the axiom which has kept
My father's summer shadowy and sweet.

Remembering many times when he has laughed
Softly, and slapped his thigh, because the trap
So suavely set was consummately sprung,
I wish, to all I love, his love of craft.

Hard to instruct myself, and then my son,
That things which would be natural are done
After a style less consummate; that art's
More noble office is to leave half-done.

How soon the shadows fall, how soon and long!
The score-board stretches to a grandson's feet.
This layabout July in another climate
Ought not to prove firm turf, well-tended, wrong.
(C.P. p. 137)

The attempted urbanity of *Brides of Wisdom* and *A Winter Talent* (1957) gives way to this humane provincialism which owes as much to Peredelkino, Pasternak's country home, as it does to Barnsley Cricket Club.

It is a pity that Pasternak is so difficult of access for the English reader. Something of his importance for Davie can be gleaned from the anthology of essays on the poet which he edited with Angela

Livingstone, and from which I have quoted. But of course, the sound and the peculiar idiom of the Russian poet must escape the reader who has no Russian. So let me finally take an English poet whose example has also been important for Davie, who in some lights can be compared with Pasternak, and with whose greatness we all have some familiarity — Wordsworth.

To invoke that name is at once to see the qualities which are absent in Davie. His poetry, it seems to me, lacks a sense of the religious; and though he is not averse to thinking in his poetry there is no *stretch* of thought we could compare, say, with 'Tintern Abbey'. And though Wordsworth is famous for his egotism and Davie populates his poems with his family and his friends, it is Wordsworth who strikes one as seeing more deeply into the individual nature. There is, too, enough of the prophet in Wordsworth to allow us to see the necessary short-comings of fairmindedness. The positive Wordsworthian aspect of Davie lies in his subject-matter and in his manner of being dramatically lyrical.

I have said that Davie's subject-matter is drawn from the mobility of our present western civilisation. The poems that I have quoted all reflect this in one way or another. He has treated the subject in ways I have been unable to illustrate. *A Sequence for Francis Parkman* (1961), for example, is a set of seven poems with a later pendant, on the discovery and settlement of North America; and there are further poems about discovery and exploration in *Six Epistles to Eva Hesse* (1970), a not wholly successful attempt at 'heroic comedy', and in *Collected Poems 1950-1970*. None of this sounds particularly Wordsworthian. And yet:

> It was English poetry (with Wordsworth) that in modern times first expressed ideas of elemental sanctity and natural piety: and it seems it must be English poetry which asks what to do with these ideas in a landscape where virtually all the sanctuaries have been violated, all the pieties blasphemed.
>
> (Davie: *Thomas Hardy and British Poetry,* 1973, p.72.)

In so far as Davie is concerned with 'elemental sanctity and natural piety' in a landscape where 'all the sanctuaries have been violated' (we can all imagine what 'Abbeyforde' looks like), he is extending a central

Wordsworthian theme in a natural fashion. The author of ' "Abbeyforde" ' is, then, Wordsworthian, and the same Wordsworthian light shines around such a poem as 'Middlesex'. (This comes from *The Shires* (1974) — a book pretty generally misunderstood (eg. TLS), but whose intention is very fully glossed by the passage just quoted):

> *Germans, she said, were sometimes independent;*
> *Her countrymen were all for package-tours,*
> *A girl from Wembley Stadium serving beers*
> *In a Greek bar. A maxiskirt from Bristol*
> *Hawked prints on the Acropolis; from Chepstow*
> *Another served us in a coffee-bar.*
>
> *Our age-group is dependent, but not theirs.*
> *Temporary drop-outs or true wives*
> *To young and struggling Greeks, they do us more*
> *Credit than we deserve, their timid parents.*
>
> *The longer loop their Odysseys, the more*
> *Warmly exact the Ithakas they remember:*
> *Thus, home she said was Middlesex, though Wembley*
> *I should have named, indifferently, as 'London'.*

This poem celebrates elemental sanctity as convincingly as ' "Abbeyforde" ' does natural piety in the age of the western diaspora.

Davie is Wordsworthianly dramatic. I used the word 'dramatic' of the latter poem — legitimately, I think, though you may disagree. At any rate, I take as my warrant a passage from one of Wordsworth's letters (19 April 1808) which crops up more than once in Davie's writing. Wordsworth disdains the 'gross and visible action' of the stage, urging the 'man of genius' ('if the Poet is to be predominant over the Dramatist') in this fashion:

> let him see if there are no victories in the world of the spirit, no changes, no connections, no revolutions there, no fluxes and refluxes of the thoughts which may be made interesting by modest combination with the stiller actions of the bodily frame, or with the gentler movements and milder appearances of society and social intercourse, or the still more mild and gentle solicitations of irrational and inanimate nature.

A poem like 'House-martin', from *Events and Wisdoms,* is illuminated just as much by that passage as by any reference to Pasternak:

> *I see the low black wherry*
> *Under the alders rock,*
> *As the ferryman strides from his ferry*
> *And his child in its black frock*
>
> *Into his powerful shadow*
> *And out of it, skirmishing, passes*
> *Time and again as they go*
> *Up through the tall lush grasses.*
>
> *The light of evening grieves*
> *For the stout house of a father,*
> *With martins under its eaves,*
> *That cracks and sags in the weather.*
> *(C.P.* 138)

Pound; Pasternak; the English eighteenth century; Wordsworth. The real poets take their place with their masters, true both to their own day and to a tradition. Donald Davie is one of them.

Agenda

Poems from Magazines
1976-1977

I

Strange room, from this angle:
white door open before me,
strange bed, mechanical hum, white lights.
There will be stranger rooms to come.

As I almost slept I saw the deep flower opening
and leaned over into it, gratefully.
It swimmingly closed in my face. I was not ready.
It was not death, it was acceptance.

Our thin patient cat died purring,
her small triangular head tilted back,
the nurse's fingers caressing her throat,
my hand on her shrunken spine; the quick needle.

That was the second death by cancer.
The first is not for me to speak of.
It was telephone-calls and brave letters
and a friend's hand bleeding under the coffin.

Doctor, I am not afraid of a word.
But neither do I wish to embrace that visitor,
to engulf it as Hine-Nui-te-Po
engulfed Maui; that would be the way of it.

And she was the winner there: her womb crushed him.
Goddesses can do these things.
But I have admitted the gloved hands and the speculum
and must part my ordinary legs to the surgeon's knife.

II

Nellie has only one breast
ample enough to make several.
Her quilted dressing-gown softens
to semi-doubtful this imbalance
and there's no starched vanity
in our floppy abundant ward-mother:
her streaked silvery hair's in braids,
her slippers loll, her weathered, classical
features hold a long, true smile.
When she dresses up in her black
with her glittering marcasite brooch on
to go for the weekly radium treatment
she's the bright star of the taxi-party —
whatever may be growing under her ribs.

Doris hardly smokes in the ward —
and hardly eats more than a dreamy spoonful —
but the corridors and bathrooms
reek of her Players number 10,
and the drug-trolley pauses
for long minutes by her bed.
Each week for the taxi-outing
she puts on her skirt again
and has to pin the slack waistband
more tightly over her scarlet sweater.
Her face, a white shadow through smoked glass,
lets Soho display itself unregarded.

Third in the car is Mrs Golding
who never smiles. And why should she?

III

The senior consultant on his rounds
murmurs in so subdued a voice

to the students marshalled behind
that they gather in, forming a cell,
a cluster, a rosette around him
as he stands at the foot of my bed
going through my notes with them,
half-audibly instructive, grave.

The slight ache as I strain forward
to listen still seems imagined.

Then he turns his practised smile on me:
'How are you this morning?' 'Fine,
very well, thank you.' I smile too.
And possibly all that murmurs within me
is the slow dissolving of stitches.

IV

I am out in the supermarket, choosing —
this very afternoon, this day —
picking up tomatoes, cheese, bread,

things I want and shall be using
to make myself a meal, while they
eat their stodgy suppers in bed —

Janet with her big freckled breasts,
her prim Scots voice, her one friend,
and never in hospital before,

who came in to have a few tests
and now can't see where they'll end;
and Coral in the bed by the door

who whimpered and gasped behind a screeen
with nurses to and fro all night
and far too much of the day;

pallid, bewildered, nineteen.
And Mary, who will be all right
but gradually. And Alice, who may.

Whereas I stand almost intact,
giddy with freedom, not with pain.
I lift my light basket, observing

how little I needed in fact;
and move to the checkout, to the rain,
to the lights and the long street curving.

The New Review

Thomas Blackburn **Francis Bacon**

The crumpled sheets of the bed of murder
You showed me how the creases, stains and folds
Make the crime perpetually occur,
The resonance and the mystery of details.

I remember the chaos of cuttings and paint,
The colours on the plate in your studio,
How you called Jesus a queen but very quaint
I disagreed but agreed with your cult of horror

And collected pictures in an old scrap book,
A dying drunk, boxers, an addict of heroin,
Many variants on the theme of pain and shock;
I shudder at them now, they were pleasant then.

Degradation, not degraded yourself, your fascination
All the varieties of misery and mania;
You called it closing in to the nerve; I leant upon
The enormity of the creature that you are

And made poems underneath your cast shadow,
Exploring the terror of bearing humanity
And relishing — what it was I still don't know,
Something about breaking out of contour into mystery.

Now at sixty-one and having learnt compassion,
Some insight from confusion and despair
I seek the pities, how to make confusion
Both in myself and others breathe fresher air

And marvel at you, very rich and famous,
Still crucified by what takes place in a bed,
And uttering, with superb technique, pretentious
Platitudes of rut, that you have said and said.

Meridian

107

The mineowner orders trees for his estate.
He wants a green substance between him
And those slagheaps black against the sun.
He cannot wait for the trees to grow
Through generations
So he has them brought to him
In wagons, roots and all.
The wagons bring the yew,
Its bark frowning at the sun;
The lime comes with a bee swarm;
The silver beech
Is followed by the lumbering oak
Whose roots hold massive fistfulls
Of earth.
And from the wagons earth falls,
And from the trees leaves fall,
And the trees are put into holes
Like vertical coffins going down.
In the morning the mineowner
Looks to the east to see the sun come up
And, yes, the slagheaps are obscured
By pillars of wood becoming coal.

Stand

I mean what
did he do? one
minute there she

was, flesh of his
flesh, hustling
along beside

him, anxious
as ice cubes to
get away from

all that fire
and justice
on the plain,

and the next
she's a pillar
of wrath—

solid salt; it
was a hell
of a price,

even if her
curiosity was
morbid; what

did he do? you
could make a
case for not

even break-
ing stride, but
after all, it

was his wife; he
may have carved
a quick R.I.P.,

not looking
back, before
goosepimpling

on, or something
more sober-
ing, like BEWARE;

she may have
become a
kind of sodium-

chloride Ozymandias;
more likely she
wound up ground

up in some
market, or licked
to a nub

by beast-tongues,
yet there's
a chance, just

a chance, the
three of them
may have carted

her along, clear
to the cave,
where, in her corner,

cool as the moon,
she whitened
all that

wine and incest,
all that girled
conniving

for the
seed, the sons,
the tribes.

The Anglo-Welsh Review

Ruth Fainlight **Divination by Hair**

I

Every few days, looking into the mirror,
I find another dozen hairs turned white.
Though dubious about my purpose, almost
despising myself, I go on pulling them out.
She, the ideal I stubbornly adhere to,
would never search so urgently for their wiry
glint, crane her neck awkwardly
the better to ensure not one escapes
the tweezer; she would disdain pursuit of such
discoveries. White hairs are curlier
and vigorous, age and death becoming
more assertive the closer they approach.

I know it can be nothing but a losing
battle, paltry and ridiculous.
Sooner or later I'll have to choose whether
to be bald or white. I cannot continue
this depilation with impunity.
They'll never grow back as fast as vanity
can raze them. As if enthralled (it cannot
be mere scrutiny distorts my face)
hours at a time I stand in front of my mirror,
which long before now should have lost its power
and become a superseded altar, not
the secret place of panic, rage, and grief.

I'd prefer to be brave, to let my tresses fade
to mottled grey and white —but even the best
resolutions are hard to keep when every
day's attrition brings a new defeat.
If only it could happen overnight:
one morning I would wake transformed into
that dignified wise matron of my dreams,
matured at last to grace — though I make her sound
like the grandmother on a birthday card,

not at all what I mean (how to convey
the essence of a person realised?) —
storms calmed, reefs passed, safe harbour now in sight.

II

Every day, new hairs faded.
Why don't I just accept it?
Why don't I dye it? What difference
would it make if I left them? Age
would not come sooner, nor my actions
avert dissolution and death.
Who do I think I'm fooling?
— No-one except myself.
For who cares really whether
my hair is grey, white, or black?
I share the general anguish.
Like others, I try my best
to conceal, refuse, forget.

III

Because death always seemed a mother —
or a grandmother — someone
familiar, now I come near
the time of greying hair, I fear
the mask more than the skull beneath.

IV

Silver hair is the warning sign.
To watch it spread is like catching fire.
I want to smother it, to hide
the mark that shows I'm next in line,
exposed, too near the danger-zone.

I feel death creeping up behind.
Those fading hairs and deepening lines
are the entangling net she throws.

V

Witch from an ancient forest-tale;
goddess; hag; Atropos-Fate;
Kali; crone. Can I placate
you better by carefully hiding the blaze
you sear across my brow, or aping
your style? Conquering queen, your embrace
is inexorable. Whether I hate
or deny or adore you, you will unmake
me, eternally, and create me again.

VI

          days   mirror
                  dozen hairs   white
   dubious purpose
despising
   ideal   stubbornly adhere
                 urgently
                 awkwardly
             not one escapes
                   pursuit
discoveries
   vigorous age and death
     assertive   approach
                       losing
    battle   paltry   ridiculous
                        choose
     bald or white
            impunity

                                    vanity
                    enthralled
                scrutiny distorts
                                        my mirror
                                    lost its power
                    a superseded altar
                        panic, rage, and grief

                    brave   tresses
            mottled grey and white   best
        resolutions
                    attrition   defeat
                            overnight
                                transformed
                    dignified   dreams
                            grace
                    grandmother
                                how convey
                essence
                    calmed   passed   harbour in sight

                                                Bananas

                                    115

I

Not my best side, I'm afraid.
The artist didn't give me a chance to
Pose properly, and as you can see,
Poor chap, he had this obsession with
Triangles, so he left off two of my
Feet. I didn't comment at the time
(What, after all, are two feet
To a monster?) but afterwards
I was sorry for the bad publicity.
Why, I said to myself, should my conqueror
Be so ostentatiously beardless, and ride
A horse with a deformed neck and square hoofs?
Why should my victim be so
Unattractive as to be inedible,
And why should she have me literally
On a string? I don't mind dying
Ritually, since I always rise again,
But I should have liked a little more blood
To show they were taking me seriously.

II

It's hard for a girl to be sure if
She wants to be rescued. I mean, I quite
Took to the dragon. It's nice to be
Liked, if you know what I mean. He was
So nicely physical, with his claws
And lovely green skin, and that sexy tail,
And the way he looked at me,
He made me feel he was all ready to
Eat me. And any girl enjoys that.
So when this boy turned up, wearing machinery,
On a really *dangerous* horse, to be honest
I didn't much fancy him. I mean,

What was he like underneath the hardware?
He might have acne, blackheads or even
Bad breath for all I could tell, but the dragon —
Well, you could see all his equipment
At a glance. Still, what could I do?
The dragon got himself beaten by the boy,
And a girl's got to think of her future.

III
I have diplomas in Dragon
Management and Virgin Reclamation.
My horse is the latest model, with
Automatic transmission and built-in
Obsolescence. My spear is custom-built,
And my prototype armour
Still on the secret list. You can't
Do better than me at the moment.
I'm qualified and equipped to the
Eyebrow. So why be difficult?
Don't you want to be killed and/or rescued
In the most contemporary way? Don't
You want to carry out the roles
That sociology and myth have designed for you?
Don't you realise that, by being choosy,
You are endangering job prospects
In the spear- and horse-building industries?
What, in any case, does it matter what
You want? You're in my way.

Encounter

Roy Fisher   **If I Didn't**

If I didn't dislike
mentioning works of art

I could say
the poem has always
already started, the parapet
snaking away, its grey line guarding
the football field and the sea

— the parapet
has always already started
snaking away, its grey line
guarding the football field and the sea

and under whatever progression
takes thing forward

there's always
the looking down
between the moving frames

into those other movements
made long ago or in some
irrecoverable scale
but in the same alignment
and close to recall.

Some I don't recognize,
but I believe them —

one system of crimson scaffolding,
another, of flanges —

All of them must be mine,
the way I move on:

and there I am,
half my lifetime back,
on Goodrington sands
one winter Saturday,

troubled in mind: troubled
only by Goodrington beach
under the gloom, the look of it
against its hinterland

and to be walking
acres of sandy wrack,
sodden and unstable
from one end to the other.

Poetry Wales

Richard Freeman   **Lift   Going   Down**

I enter on the seventh,
The doors close like eyelids.

Inside its metal cupboard
The emergency phone is a curled
Up black kitten.

There's a sense of danger being
Neither up nor down
Inside or out
In light or darkness
With friends or enemies.

If I were rude to the man
He'd be on the board tomorrow.
To go up or down I'd have
To press the buttons on his waistcoat.

The girl is juicy slices of hipbone,
A vegetable display
With runner beans for shadows.

When we get down, the eye
Will open. We shall be removed
With the corner of a handkerchief.

Ambit

Roy Fuller   **On Birkett Marshall's 'Rare Poems of the Seventeenth Century'**

Coppinger, Pordage, Collop, Fayne,
Fettiplace, Farley, Chamberlain—

They could be the darling poets of my youth:
I almost search among the names for mine.

All have remunerative occupations—
Physician, milliner, playwright, baronet!

Some are locked in a single year— "alive"
In '62 or "floruit" '39.

Nothing is known of Pick or Prestwich. Still,
What wonder life behind the poetry fades?

Three hundred years ago they were consoled
For lack of genius and fame by some

Astonishing trope or stanza's tailoring.
Strange that the consolation still should work

—Prujean, "Ephelia", Cutts, Cockayne,
Cameron, Allott, Fuller, Raine.

Encounter

Seamus Heaney   **Thunderlight**

Thunderlight on the split logs: big raindrops
At body heat and lush with omen
Spattering dark on the hatchet iron.
This morning, when a magpie with jerky steps
Inspected a horse asleep beside the wood
I thought of dew on armour and carrion.
What would I meet, blood-boltered, on the road?
How deep into the woodpile sat the toad?
What welters through this dark hush on the crops?
Do you remember that *pension* in Les Landes
Where the old one rocked and rocked and rocked
A mongol on her lap, to little songs?
Come to me quick. I am upstairs shaking.
My all of you birchwood in lightning.

The   Little   Word   Machine

Diana Hendry   **Funeral Dance**

The spire is as perfectly centred
as the black and white priest in the doorway's arch.
Left of centre stands a large yew.
Six staunch bearers pace the path.
On the raw oak box, the shields of flowers
are heraldic crests that mock
our claims. Outside the gates
the mourners make two half moons.

Bach could have set it as a four-part fugue
but for the two shapeless figures
in sullen grey who stumble, unsynchronised
after the coffin, breaking the dance,
draining the colour out of the grass,
making the priest seem sawdust and silk,
neutralising spire, yew tree, arch.

Encounter

Diana Hendry   **Soliloquy to a Belly**

I have grown a belly.
It has swallowed up
my legs and arms,
even my head.

The government owns it.
Their man
comes to examine it
regularly,
like the meter.
I say "I am behind it",
but he has his union,

123

he has his schedule.

The old mothers
have come to my bedroom
to keep their vigil.
They sit and knit
straitjackets for daughters.
It's the species that matter,
it's all quite natural;
little husk,
you're for corn.

Along the street
the no-bellies walk.
In the space between
their breasts and legs
they've a squeeze
of desire, like picnic salt
in a twist of paper.
They'd like a belly
to sleep behind.

I'm afraid
my arms and legs
won't grow again.
It happens every day of the week,
you're not unique,
not even special.

I'll hem my sheets,
I'll let them read the meter twice,
I'll be nice to the midwife,
push when I'm told.
I'm lying in
behind this belly,
thin and cold.

Stroud Festival

124

Molly Holden   **Stopping Places**

The long car journeys to the sea
must have their breaks, not always
in towns where there's no room
to park but at the pavement's edge,
in villages, or by the woods, or in lay-bys
vibrating to the passage of fast cars.
The seat's pushed forward, the boot's lifted,
the greaseproof paper
rustles encouragingly. The children
climb to the ground and posture about,
talk, clamber on gates, eat noisily.
They're herded back, the journey
continues.
    What do you think
they'll remember most of that holiday?
the beach? the stately home?
the hot kerb of the promenade?
No. It will often be those nameless places
where they stopped, perhaps for no more
than minutes. The rank grass
and the dingy robin by the overflowing
bin for waste, the gravel ridged by
numerous wheels and the briared wood
that no one else had bothered
to explore, the long inviting field
down which there wasn't time
to go — these will stick in their memories
when beauty spots evaporate.
Was it worth the expense?
                              but
these are the rewards of travelling.
There must be an end in sight
for the transient stopping places
to be necessary, to be memorable.

The Honest Ulsterman

A lamb could not get born. Ice wind
Out of a downpour dishclout sunrise. The mother
Lay on the mudded slope. Harried, she got up
And the blackish lump bobbed at her back-end
Under her tail. After some hard galloping,
Some manoeuvring, much flapping of the backward
Lump head of the lamb looking out,
I caught her with a rope. Laid her, head uphill
And examined the lamb. A blood-ball swollen
Tight in its black felt, its mouth gap
Squashed crooked, tongue stuck out, black-purple,
Strangled by its mother. I felt inside,
Past the noose of mother-flesh, into the slippery
Muscled tunnel, fingering for a hoof,
Right back to the port-hole of the pelvis.
But there was no hoof. He had stuck his head out too
And his feet could not follow. He should have
Felt his way, tip-toe, his toes
Tucked up under his nose
For a safe landing. So I kneeled wrestling
With her groans. No hand could squeeze past
The lamb's neck into her interior
To hook a knee. I roped that head
And hauled till she cried out and tried
To get up and I saw it was useless. I went
Two miles for the injection and a razor.
Sliced the lamb's throat-strings, levered with a knife
Between the vertebrae and brought the head off,
To stare at its mother, its pipe sitting in the mud
With all earth for a body. Then pushed
The neck-stump right back in, and as I pushed
She pushed. She pushed crying and I pushed gasping.
And the strength
Of the birth push and the push of my thumb
Against that wobbly vertebra were deadlock,

A to-fro futility. Till I forced
A hand past and got a knee. Then like
Pulling myself to the ceiling with one finger
Hooked in a loop, timing my effort
To her birth push groans, I pulled against
The corpse that would not come. Till it came.
And after it the long, sudden, yolk-yellow
Parcel of life
In a smoking slither of oils and soups and syrups —
And the body lay born, beside the hacked-off head.

Bananas

Nigel Jenkins **First Calving**

Up through the rain I'd driven her, taut
hocks out-sharing a streak of the caul,
and that single hoof, pale as lard,
poked out beneath her tail.

In shelter,
across the yard from me now,
her rump's whiteness fretted the dark.
I watched there the obscure passage
of men's hands and, exiled in crass
daylight, waited—

                      till a shout
sent me running big with purpose
to the stable for a halter.

They flipped to me the rope's end, its
webbing they noosed around the hoof:
we leaned there, two of us, lending weight
to each contraction; the other fumbled
for the drowning muzzle, the absent leg,
   said he'd heard that over Betws way
       some farmer'd done this with a tractor—
          pulled the calf to bits and killed the cow

Again she pushed, and to first air
we brought the nostrils free; next the head
and blockaging shoulders, then out
he flopped, lay there like some bones pudding,
steaming with life.

           Later,
she cleansed. I grubbed a hole in the earth
and carried the afterbirth out
on a shovel: to be weighted with a stone,
they said, to keep it from the scavengers.

The Anglo-Welsh Review

Brian Jones   **The Island Normal**

So often we push off from it, bored stiff
by its rightness, taking ages to jettison
the blue prescription of its near-shore waters,
and in no time we know we've insufficient
stomach for the great swell, and our bark
is far from noble, and should we both
flop and disappear, few will remember, fewer mourn.
It's the getting back that's miraculous.
It's really miraculous — chartless, inept,
working only at the next swell, the next buffet of-wind,
we're hopeless. Then up it heaves, the Island,
as if anchored and full of compassion.
Back over that bay, its blues suddenly gorgeous,
stepping onto the jetty, the wood creaking,
we're primed, it feels, like Odysseus with marvels.
But since we've been nowhere, precisely Nowhere,
of all those quiet Normalists, who shore-based know
the obvious horrors of ocean, who will listen?

London Magazine

Brian Jones   **Overnight**

Stopping somewhere in England at a place
nondescript, halfway to our intention,
we get a bed, and garage the hot car,
lugging only the one white case upstairs
to a room we barely look at.
We eat what's here and pass no comment —
it's chance, after all, that we've alighted
between the poles of choice. But look at her face
who carries plates to us and responds
to what must be a child howling somewhere

129

in whatever part is private in this house.
She also is smiling, since it doesn't matter,
but going from the room has all the swift
compulsion of the really trapped.
We glimpse again all those momentous wheres
we're always absent from, as when
the train unscheduled stops, or the tyre
flattens in an irrelevant street. But not
tonight the normal rate of jettison.
We lie later actually studying the room,
someone's taste of paper and curtaining, someone's
odd aside of a landscape, raw, unframed;
restlessly sleepless on futile snags of question,
who have come in from the night to feel exclusion.

London Magazine

Brian Jones   **Too Late**

All those old crap songs poking their heads
round the blind alleys we walk and wringing
the nearest thing to tears from these dry hearts.
The air of putrefaction when the bar raises
its Sunday voice in 'I'll take you home again
Kathleen' and we all want to drape our arms
round everybody's neck and say 'Yes, that's how . . .'
and waking with gritty head on Monday reading
another child is dead with its plastic gun.
Forgive our trespasses. We have many trespasses.
We're all doing our worst down the wrong
road, and the crap songs and Little Nell's foul death
jerk our sickness weepy. Sirens are calling us,
miles away, long sailed-past, long-refused.
Achilles shagged Penthesilea when she was dead.
Rightly, we felt revulsion. We understand.

London Magazine

Golden-hooved
the sun beat down
hammered us into silence
Skins in subtle unity
thin as foil.

Naked & high
surrounded by
curious beasts
both mythic & real
we stared back

released from flesh & fear
seeing them for the first time
on such a level.
Eye to eye.

Until, aware
of the vulnerable
linked solitude
of living things

they moved away,
pounded the warming earth
to leave us be
within that rare

gold radiance where
we lay.

Derek Mahon   **A True Story**

Early in the spring of nineteen forty-four
Planes of the Royal Air Force
Dropped, in preparation for D-Day
And the big advance,
Poems by Paul Eluard
On the dark fields of France.

Down they went through the moonlight,
The poems of Paul Eluard,
Twirling like sycamore leaves
In the mild sky, to alight
Not in this field
Or the next, but the one after.

The pilots whistled 'We'll Meet Again'
High above the winding Seine.
Few of them were habitual readers of poetry
And fewer still were familiar
With the work of Paul Eluard.
Nor were the milkmaids and railwaymen
Who picked the poems up
And studied them over their morning cup
Of *café au lait*
Much more *au fait*.

Eluard himself was asleep in his Paris studio
While this was going on
And must have been startled to learn
Of his overnight fame when he turned on the radio.

D-Day after some initial setbacks, worked out fine.
The milkmaids married the railwaymen.
Eluard died eight years later of an embolism,
A prophet in his own country,
Having abandoned surrealism,

His original commitment,
For a more direct kind of statement.

But pity the pilots, young men from Guildford
And Colchester who, trained to bounce
Bombs on Berlin and Dresden, scattered
Poems instead to the quiet winds of France.
In pavilions, golf clubs, and the lounge bar
Of the 'Dog and Car'
They hide their faces for shame
In their halves of bitter,
Remembering what *they* did in the war —
Not pounding the fucking Huns
But contributing to the greater glory of Paul Eluard.

The Honest Ulsterman

His bones are red from lady's bedstraw.
He is fed, too, according to season,
Dry meadow-rue, juiceless rest-harrow.

Enchanter's nightshade made him docile.
He was led abject, pathetic
In jewelled collar, into this palisade.

The stains on his flanks are not of blood;
The bursting pomegranates spill their seeds
From the tree where he's tethered.

He day-dreams of jack-by-the-hedge, lances
Of goldenrod to crunch on, tangled
Heart's ease, salads of nipple-wort.

His nightmares are acres of fool's parsley.
He wakes hungry for self-heal
And the clingings of traveller's joy.

Released in winter, he does not stray.
The tip of his horn a blind periscope,
He trembles in sweet dung under deep snow.

The Anglo-Welsh Review

Everyone's got someone who gave them oranges,
Sovereigns or rubbed florins,
Who wore bottle-green blazers, smoked
A churchwarden pipe on St. Swithun's day,
And mulled their ale by dousing red-hot pokers
In quart jars.
But you, you're different.
You pushed off before the millions wrapped their puttees on
And ran away to sea, the prairies, New York
Where they threw you in jail when you told someone
Your blond hair made you a German spy.
After the telegram demanding
Your birth certificate
No one on the Island knew anything about you
Until the Armistice brought a letter
From a wife they'd never heard of.
You'd left her with the baby.
She wanted money.
You were somewhere in South America
In the greatest freedom, the freedom
Of nothing-was-ever-heard-of-him-since.

So I see you sometimes
Paddling up the Orinoco or the River Plate
With rifle, trusty mongrel and native mistress,
Passing cities of abandoned stucco
Draped with lianas and anacondas,
Passing their derelict opera houses
Where Caruso used to warble
Among a million bottles of imported bubbly.
Or else I watch you among the packing-case republics,
Drinking rum at the seafront in Buenos Aires
And waiting for your luck to change;
The warm sticky nights, the news from Europe,
Then the war criminals settling like bats

In the greasy darkness.
Your sister thought she saw your face once
In a crowd scene—
She went to the cinema for a week, watching
For your pale moment. She thinks
You're still alive, sitting back
On the veranda of your hacienda,
My lost great uncle, the blond
Indestructible dare-devil
Who was always playing truant and jumping
Off the harbour wall.

What I want to know is
How you did it.
How you threw off an inherited caution
Or just never knew it.
I think your grave is lost
In the mush of a tropical continent.
You are a memory that blipped out.
And though they named you from the king
Who's supposed to wake and come back
Some day,
I know that if you turned up on my doorstep,
An old sea dog with a worn leather belt
And a face I'd seen somewhere before,
You'd get no welcome.
I'd want you away.

The Honest Ulsterman

In wet May, in the months of change,
In a country you wouldn't visit, strange
Dreams pursue me in my sleep,
Black creatures of the upper deep—
Though you are five months dead, I see
You in guilt's iconography.
Dear wife, lost beast, beleagured child,
The stranded monster with the mild
Appearance, whom small waves tease,
(Andromeda upon her knees
In orthodox deliverance)
And you alone of pure substance
The unformed form of life, the earth
Which Piero's brushes brought to birth
For all to greet as myth, a thing
Out of the box of imagining.

This introduction serves to sing
Your mortal death as Bishop King
Once hymned in tetrametric rhyme
His young wife, lost before her time;
Though he lived on for many years
His poem each day fed new tears
To that unreaching spot, her grave,
His lines a baroque architrave
The Sunday poor with bottled flowers,
Would by-pass in their mourning hours
Esteeming ragged natural life
('Most dearly loved, most gentle wife'),
Yet, looking back when at the gate
And seeing grief in formal state
Upon a sculpted angel group,
Were glad that men of god could stoop
To give the dead a public stance
And freeze them in their mortal dance.

The words and faces proper to
My misery are private — you
Would never share your heart with those
Whose only talent's to suppose,
Nor from your final childish bed
Raise a remote confessing head —
The channels of our lives are blocked,
The hand is stopped upon the clock,
No-one can say why hearts will break
And marriages are all opaque;
A map of loss, some posted cards,
The living house reduced to shards,
The abstract hell of memory,
The pointlessness of poetry —
These are the instances which tell
Of something which I know full well:
I owe a death to you — one day
The time will come for me to pay
When your slim shape from photographs
Stands at my door and gently asks
If I have any work to do
Or will I come to bed with you.
O scala enigmatica,
I'll climb up to that attic where
The curtain of your life was drawn
Some time between despair and dawn—
I'll never know with what halt steps
You mounted to this plain eclipse
But each stair now will station me
A black responsibility
And point me to that shut-down room,
'This be your due appointed tomb.'

I think of us in Italy:
Gin-and-chianti-fuelled, we
Move in a trance through Paradise,
Feeding at last our starving eyes,
Two people of the English blindness

138

Doing each masterpiece the kindness
Of discovering it — from Baldovinetti
To Venice's most obscure jetty —
A true unfortunate traveller, I
Depend upon your nurse's eye
To pick the altars where no Grinner
Puts us off our tourists' dinner
And in hotels to bandy words
With Genevan girls and talking birds,
To wear your feet out following me
To night's end and true amity,
And call my rational fear of flying
A paradigm of Holy Dying —
And, oh my love, I wish you were
Once more with me, at night somewhere
In narrow streets applauding wines,
The moon above the Appenines
As large as logic and the stars,
Most middle-aged of avatars,
As bright as when they shone for truth
Upon untried and avid youth.
The rooms and days we wandered through
Shrink in my mind to one — there you
Lie quite absorbed by peace — the calm
Which life could not provide is balm
In death. Unseen by me, you look
Past bed and stairs and half-read book
Eternally upon your home,
The end of pain, the left alone:
I have no friend, or intercessor,
No psychopomp or true confessor
But only you who know my heart
In every cramped and devious part —
Then take my hand and lead me out,
The sky is overcast by doubt,
The time has come, I listen for
Your words of comfort at the door,

O guide me through the shoals of fear —
'Fürchte dich nicht, ich bin bei dir.'

Quadrant

Peter Porter   **An Angel in Blythburgh Church**

Shot down from its enskied formation,
This stern-faced plummet rests against the wall;
Cromwell's soldiers peppered it and now the death-
     watch beetle has it in thrall.

If you make fortunes from wool, along
The weeping winter foreshores of the tide,
You build big churches with clerestories
     And place angels high inside.

Their painted faces guard and guide. Now or
Tomorrow or whenever is the promise—
The resurrection comes: fix your eyes halfway
     Between Heaven and Diss.

The face is crudely carved, simplified by wind;
It looks straight at God and waits for orders,
Buffeted by the organ militant, and blasted
     By choristers and recorders.

Faith would have our eyes as wooden and as certain.
It might be worth it, to start the New Year's hymn
Allowing for death as a mere calculation,
     A depreciation, entered in.

Or so I fancy looking at the roof beams
Where the dangerous beetle sails. What is it
Turns an atheist's mind to prayer in almost
    Any church on a country visit?

Greed for love or certainty or forgiveness?
High security rising with the sea birds?
A theology of self-looking for precedents?
    A chance to speak old words?

Rather, I think of a woman lying on her bed
Staring for hours up to the ceiling where
Nothing is projected — death the only angel
    To shield her from despair.

Encounter

Peter Porter   **The Easiest Room in Hell**

At the top of the stairs is a room
one may speak of only in parable.

It is the childhood attic,
the place to go when love has worn away,
the origin of the smell of self.

We came here on a clandestine visit
and in the full fire of indifference.

We sorted out books and let the children
sleep here away from creatures.

From its windows, ruled by willows,
the flatlands of childhood stretched
to the watermeadows.

It was the site of a massacre,
of the running down of the body
to less even than the soul,
the tribe's revenge on everything.

It was the heart of England
where the ballerinas were on points
and locums laughed through every evening.

Once it held all the games,
Inconsequences, Misalliance, Frustration,
Even *Mendacity, Adultery* and *Manic Depression.*

But that was just its alibi,
all along it was home,
a home away from home.

Having such a sanctuary
we who parted here
will be reunited here.

You asked in an uncharacteristic note,
"Dwell I but in the suburbs
of your good pleasure?"

I replied: "To us has been allowed
the easiest room in hell."

Once it belonged to you,
now it is only mine.

Encounter

Elizabeth Saxon   **Bedtime**

He'd usually come back from the pub drunk.
I'd hear his feet on the path,
then his boot on the door with a crash.
Bending over me, his braces straining across his chest
he'd pull my ear saying "Bed, boy!"
I'd hear them shouting as I went to sleep.

I should have learnt to keep out of the way.
I never did, for sometimes, bleary eyed,
he'd fling a scratchy bag of crisps across,
then turn and pull my mother down,
the sofa shedding knitting on the floor.
A large hand pointed to the door.
I hurried off and up the stairs,
eating the crisps slowly in little bits,
saving the salt till last.

Poetry Wales

A walk in Central Park,
New York friends tell me, is far from being a lark.
If lucky enough to escape attack by muggers
You will attract the more insidious attentions of buggers.
At night it is even more dangerous than the subways,
Those hubways
Of delinquency and violence.
                              But I walked there at dusk
and felt as safe as if I were in the office of Dean Rusk.
It is a city park, hard cracked and bare
And melancholy, like the brown bear
Who paws at his cage in the Zoo. In places the grass
Looks as if it has received attention from (to quote
                    Cummings) Lil's white arse.
The lamps are wired over to prevent their destruction
And boys playing baseball are warned: 'Instruction,
Use soft ball only.' The cars move through it, spat out
                    by the great suction
Cleaner on West, sucked in again on East. Trees, greenness
                    are incidental,
For this park is part of the roaring mental
Delirium of the city. Although the prospects please
The park is a place of excitement, not ease.
It is this, and not the assaults of sluggers and huggers
That make a walk in Central Park,
In daylight or after dark,
Something short of a lark.

London Magazine

I. P. Taylor   **August Ritual**

Twenty-two hundred acres —
and every hand is needed. They'd hire
a lunatic, if he could sweat, go black
in the dustswirl, stamp
on a bucking Five Thousand.

Three abreast, the revolving jaws
jam down. The raised blades roar on the turn,
mill flies and plunge back. Nothing escapes
from the falling horizon: rabbits minced
to string, stones bounced head-high.

The afternoon swelters. Activity shimmers
like a foundry with the roof off.
Diesel scorches air to brassy cloudlessness.

At dusk, the carnival dies
to grotesque silhouette. Metal ticks and cools.
Tractors, like old locomotives,
exhale steam. Voices, stranded about the field,
lift on small evening winds.

Tactics are agreed. The engines
shatter out again. Trailers, diesel-tank,
elevators, chocks, trundle across the dale.
Tomorrow the ninety acre — pounded
bare as a Brahmin's skull.

One month and it's done: the combines
backed under the widespan, with a final snort
and judder of desire; the last bales up.

Stubbles gleam under narrowing light, hiss
against westerlies. And the rains—
steady water sluicing the plough.

Workshop New Poetry

Anthony Thwaite   **At the Shrine of Santa Zita**
                     (patron saint of domestic work. b. 1218,
                     d. 1278, in S. Frediano, Lucca)

What are you doing here, quiet under glass,
White frills and flowered chaplet, open mouth
Hard-beaked as a tortoise?
Your leathery hands have done with knitting, baking,
Wiping and dishwashing and mending cast-offs.
You have put your feet up.

Odd at first sight that you should be presented
Thus, like a girl dressed for her confirmation,
Weary of miracles.
Yet the brown mummy spruced so smart and tidy,
Dry skin and bones made housewifely and decent,
Is a true emblem.

Seven hundred years of labour-saving gadgets
Weigh little in the balance put against you,
Gaunt patroness of habit.
It would be pleasant if such daily order,
Such steady working at routines and drudging,
Were always framed so.

Parcelling up the garbage for collection,
We catch the reek of everything neglected
Shoved into corners.
The sweeper-up we do not care to mention
Sets to his chores more ruthlessly than you did,
And sifts no rubbish.

But here you lie in your ridiculous canopy,
An old crone in a little girl's white finery,
Your left hand resting
Restlessly on the lace, as if impatient
To pick a rag up from the floor beside you
And go on dusting.
                                        Encounter

146

Charles Tomlinson   **The Shaft**

The shaft seemed like a place of sacrifice:
You climbed where spoil heaps from the hill
Spilled out into a wood, the slate
Tinkling underfoot like shards, and then
You bent to enter: a passageway:
Cervix of stone: the tick of waterdrops,
A clear clepsydra: and squeezing through
Emerged into cathedral space, held-up
By a single rocksheaf, a gerbe
Buttressing-back the roof. The shaft
Opened beneath it, all its levels
Lost in a hundred feet of water.
Those miners — dust, beards, mattocks —
They photographed seventy years ago,
Might well have gone to ground here, pharaohs
Awaiting excavation, their drowned equipment
Laid-out beside them. All you could see
Was rock reflections tunnelling the floor
That water covered, a vertical unfathomed,
A vertigo that dropped through centuries
To the first who broke into these fells:
The shaft was not a place to stare into
Or not for long: the adit you entered by
Filtered a leaf-light, a phosphorescence,
Doubled by water to a tremulous fire
And signalling you back to the moist door
Into whose darkness you had turned aside
Out of the sun of an unfinished summer.

Times Literary Supplement

Lives of the Poets

When Brendan Behan became famous he had to prove it to himself every day, and others had to repeat continually that it was so. Of course the people from whom such recognitions could never be extracted were those from whom he most wanted them. The possibilities of fame as an instrument of power over others are limited to those who admit its importance, which serious fellow-artists rarely do.

Kavanagh's hostility was implacable and, instead of accepting this, Brendan went about the town creating a sort of intimacy with him by abuse, constantly talking in abusive terms about anybody to third parties being of course one of the best known means of remaining close to them that there is. Now to add to his troubles came the Kavanagh libel action, which, even if it provided him with an obscure and unsatisfactory sort of revenge, reduced his stock still further among the two or three whose respect he most wanted.

Like all Irish countrymen, Kavanagh was highly litigious. He had a great respect for legal forms and phrases and he would often use them in ordinary conversation, accurately or inaccurately, in or out of context. If you taught him a new one, or he picked one up, he would use it for weeks. Worse still, he had the Irish countryman's dream of a bonanza thrown up by an action. In the case of simple folk this takes the form of dreams about damages for personal injury, breach of promise, trespass and whatnot. Kavanagh, being a literary man, dreamed of libel. And, unfortunately for himself, he was libelled. An old-established but attenuated weekly called *The Leader* was rouging its aged cheeks and decided to do a series of sophisticated profiles of contemporary personalities. Among them was Kavanagh.

The piece itself was a typical example of a certain kind of Dublin bad manners, but it was scarcely any more. Dublin is the administrative capital of a small country with a swollen civil service. It is also a University city twice over. Academics and civil servants are frequently of a literary bent, but they are rarely real writers. Dublin therefore contains some hundreds of uncreative literary men, most of them recruited from the provinces, and liberated from provincial backgrounds of varying remoteness. To be able to exchange literary gossip, to be 'in' becomes essential for them. The piece complained of was an exercise in a sort of 'innishness' that is highly offensive, but, *sub specie aeternitatis*, not very important.

Unfortunately, besides being litigious by nature, Paddy had a well-sharpened appetite for martyrdom. I understood why in part even then, but I understand better now. There is in every human being a desire for the explainable, clear-cut, black and white circumstance on which we can bring the more obvious emotions about justice and injustice to bear. Paddy was, in a very real sense, the victim of society, but, apart from the suppression of *The Great Hunger* many years before, it was hard to point to any overt act of persecution.

He was largely derided and certainly unsupported, but this, unless in a reasoned indictment of society for its sins of omission, did not amount to a crime against him. His circumstances were almost as bad as were those of many who suffered overt persecution in Russia and elsewhere; indeed, as a consequence, he used to speak with scorn of such writers and their fashionable sympathisers; yet, in his case, there was no actual persecution or dramatic martyrdom to point to. Without perhaps realising it therefore, he decided to bring all his inchoate feelings about this to a head through the medium of a libel action. He decided in fact to achieve martyrdom, and, up to a point, he succeeded brilliantly. By the time he was in the witness box being cross-examined about his character, general reputation and way of life, by the former Prime Minister, John A. Costello, it had been largely forgotten by himself, by his supporters and by the general public that he was the instigator of the action. With a sort of subliminal strategic genius he had succeeded in bringing the whole thing full circle. Like Oscar before him — who of course was also the instigator of the original action — he had become the persecuted one, and before it was over hung high on his cross for all to see, answering his persecutors disdainfully through bleeding lips.

There was one further aspect of the affair, small in itself, which was made to serve the persecution complex brilliantly also. The article was anonymous. This did not seem to me to matter very greatly unless on a personal level, or unless the lawyers could succeed in proving malice, but it was all Paddy needed to link whole segments of the town in a conspiracy against him. It gradually began to be borne in on me that as far as persecution feelings were concerned he was pretty far gone. Aided by whiskey, of which he was not drinking large quantities, and an illness, cancer of the lung, which was as yet undiagnosed, the imaginings of persecution flourished.

For weeks preliminary to the trial one was compelled to engage in speculation as to who had written the offending piece. He would ring me up at *The Bell,* which, bound by some unalterable law of return, I was now editing yet again, and, dropping his voice to the hoarse bellow that passed for conspiratorial tones, begin.

'I say. You know that piece.'

One did of course.

'I've been thinking it over. I was thinking about it all night. I've been putting two and two together.'

There would be a pause here during which one had to make some sound, for he was the most demanding of interlocutors on the telephone, requiring responses even to his silences.

'Do you know what my opinion is, my considered opinion?'

Since he had had several over the last forty-eight hours one could only say something weak like, 'No, what is it?'

'My opinion is that that blackguard so-and-so wrote it.'

This was very likely a name that had already been discussed at length so you could only repeat what you had said the night before. Of course if it was a new name, it was easier to comment; but some of the suggested names were simply beyond discussion.

At length Paddy decided that the piece had been written by *(a)* a University College Dublin historian or *(b)* a well-known civil servant poet or *(c)* both of them together.

But something else suggesting conspiracy was necessary and this was found. The piece was mainly concerned with the *persona* Paddy presented to the world in McDaid's and it had occasional gleams of accuracy as to his line of chat and general demeanour. Therefore a McDaid's informant was postulated. This role was allotted to Behan. Whichever of them had written it, if either of them had written it, or if it had been written by them both jointly, Behan had been the 'informer'. Further Behan was being paid by the opposition to follow him round at a distance and spy on him. Why particularly an informant or 'informer' had been necessary to help in the concocting of a piece which even the most amateur of journalists could have managed if its owner had put his head round the back door of McDaid's for five minutes, or what such an informer could hope to gain from cocking his ear to Paddy's conversation in Ryan's or Mooney's that would be of assistance to anybody in a libel action in a court of law, was never clear, but such questions no longer arose. He was now on trial for a nameless offence, in the realms of literature, philosophy and politics all at once, in fact, one might say, for mere being, and his enemies had of course to be credited with employing the traditional Irish weapons of persecution, including spies and informers. The objection, if any had the temerity to make it, that shouting inchoate abuse at a man was a funny way of spying on him was answered by the theory that Behan was also employed to upset him and make him do something foolish which could be brought out in court. The sum which Behan received was even named: ten shillings a day.

As the time of the hearing came nearer his nervousness naturally increased, as would anyone's with any temperament whatever. He asked me whether they could 'bring out' things in his past life against him. I thought this meant some unnamed foolishness or misdemeanour in his past. It turned out that to make himself slightly younger he had been giving the wrong year of birth in biographical notes for books and the occasional anthology. He had been worrying about this as well as a multiplicity of other things. Nobody with a highly developed sense of privacy or with more than the usual number of secrets to guard should ever engage in legal action. Unfortunately they are the very people who do.

As a means of raising money the trial was certainly a flop, since the jury found that there was no libel at all. However, as an exercise in martyrdom it was, up to a certain point anyway, a superb success. In this respect the other side played into Paddy's hands by engaging John A. Costello as senior counsel. Costello was a forceful, occasionally rather savage lawyer of the old school, dating back to O'Connell, a great juryman who on this occasion pretended, if that was possible, to be more ignorant of art and letters than the jury themselves, while concealing behind his pretended bafflement a mind as sharp as a knife. For Paddy's subconscious purposes he was therefore the ideal instrument and there took place between them an extraordinary dance of opposites. One was the poet, high style. The other was the plain citizen who knew nothing about such matters and was inclined to be distrustful of them. Constello could not pronounce the names of certain writers; indeed he affected to find them somehow funny; and he had never heard of *Moby Dick*. Paddy, in spite of his alleged peasant cunning and his indubitable desire for the spoils, was a vatic figure who made sometimes obscure but occasionally profound pronouncements much more suited to the bar of history than the tribunal in question. Costello kept turning to the jury with a mixture of sarcasm, condescension to 'the quare poet' and occasional winks of heavy understanding. Paddy leaned wearily down from the slopes of Parnassus to deliver his ultimate aesthetic. It was Mammon and Spirit, Philistine and Poet, even Marsyas and Apollo.

The purposes of both parties, overt or subconscious, were further served by a judge who allowed Costello to get away with what was in effect a plea of justification without actually introducing one and taking the consequences, that is to say he allowed him to cross-examine Paddy on the truth of the article's general picture of his way of life without specifically pleading that the article was true. There thus emerged a portrait which was in one light that of a 'character' who never paid for his own drink: in another that of The Poet and His Poverty-stricken Way. Both parties were happy with this. The only difference was that Costello was winning the verdict of the jury and he knew it, while Paddy was in all innocence asking for that of posterity.

Unfortunately the tone of the proceedings was somewhat lowered when he agreed that his work had been praised by Sir Desmond MacCarthy and that he was highly regarded as a Catholic journalist. It did not help either that he should reply when Costello asserted that Austin Clarke was equally highly regarded in the world of poetry: 'He's not in *The Faber Book of Twentieth Century Verse.*'

Yet by and large he maintained his role while Costello gleefully played the heavy straight man opposite him. Histrionically both parties were superb: Costello comically sharing his incomprehension with the jury; Paddy dropping pearls before swine in prolonged, nasal Monaghan vowels which gave an impression of the utmost distaste. Then across this masterly dialectic, subtle and self-contained, fell the outrageous shadow of Brendan. The gods had decided to turn high comedy into low farce.

On the fourth day Costello quietly and without apparent relevance asked him if he was a friend of Brendan Behan's. The object at that stage may only have been to associate him with somebody disreputable. No harm would have been done if Paddy had replied non-committally, or casually, or even declared that he was unfortunately acquainted with the said party. Instead he grew almost hysterical. In high and passionate tones he described Behan as a low blackguard who followed him about, shouting after him in the streets and forcing him to run away. Anybody who knew Paddy and the relationship such as it was could have testified to the truth of this picture. Unfortunately the protest was too shrill. The jury were sharp fellows. They exercised their intelligences in the only way common humanity knows how. They looked for the motive.

When I came out of the packed courtroom Brendan was, oddly enough, in the hallway. He had a heavy growth of beard, the blue suit was even more crumpled and stained than usual and the open-necked shirt was torn down the front. Whatever his role was, that of despised proleterian writer or rough diamond among the dishonest sophisticates, he was got up for it. He was also evidently drunk.

It was a surprise to see him there, for this was the first time he had been anywhere near the proceedings. He shouldered his way through a knot of people towards the outer door and towards where I was standing. I thought he was going to speak to me but he did no more than mutter something about the Monaghan bogman as he passed. I didn't want a scene, but I had hoped for more.

On the next day, early in the proceedings, Costello produced his secret weapon, his Zinoviev letter. Amid the sort of hush which pervades a courtroom when the audience realises that here at last is what it came to witness, he handed Paddy a copy of his own book *Tarry Flynn* and asked him to read the inscription on the flyleaf. It said: 'To my friend Brendan Behan on the day he painted my flat.' The effect was calamitous. The jury now had something they could understand, and they were no longer afraid. Up to that point they had been to some degree intimidated by attitudes they could no more comprehend than they could the mysteries of their own religion, but which a good deal of their conditioning had led them in some obscure way to respect. Now the god had died. Kavanagh was like themselves, a fallible mortal who tried to get away with it when he could. The broad smiles with which they witnessed his discomfiture were those of fellowship and understanding.

The book had of course no relevance whatever to the issues of the trial, but it finished Kavanagh off with the good men and true. What was worse from his own point of view was that it made him uncertain and affected adversely the Parnassian way in which he had hitherto conducted his own part of the proceedings. It was not just that he had been found out, it was that his obsession with Behan and with plots and counter-plots took over. To be too much concerned with anybody, whether through love or hate or fear, or even merely an ungovernable distaste, is to give them power over you.

In fact the moment Costello sprung his trap I had remembered the strange freak of chance that gave him the opportunity. Paddy had been destroyed by the one and only occasion, certainly more than two years before, on which he had ever allowed himself to talk to Brendan in amity. One Sunday night, towards the ultimate end of the Catacombs as a gathering place, there had been a rather nondescript party with a good deal of tuneless song and repetitive argument. At the height of the proceedings, such as they were, in came Brendan, and, to my extreme surprise, Kavanagh. That Kavanagh should have come with Brendan was incredible.

He had a way when entering any gathering of announcing his presence immediately. His was a speaking part, and everybody should know it. Immediately on entering a room or a pub he would deliver himself of this thought of the moment as if it was so exciting that he could wait no longer. On this occasion he came straight over to where I stood and said: 'I've discovered another fallacy. They were telling us lies. It's not true about oil and water. Not true at all. They do mix.' At first I thought he was talking metaphorically about himself and his companion, but it turned out that he meant literally oil and water. The discovery had been made when Behan, who was painting his flat preparatory to the arrival from America of a rich woman in whom he reposed some hopes, had used water instead of turpentine to thin out the paint. How it came about that the same fellow was allowed inside the door I could only guess. In his enthusiasm about the prospect of entertaining the lady, Paddy had evidently assented to the proposition of some third party that Behan was the very man for the job, being in the trade and able to knock off some paint — an important consideration — and Behan of course had leaped at the chance. The day was one of those islands of amity which occur when the stronger, or at

157

least the besieged, party in such a relationship weakens for the moment, nearly always to his subsequent regret. The *rapprochement,* if it can be called such, lasted for that Sunday only, but it was a Sunday which was to rise again above the waters of time, to Kavanagh's amazement and dismay. On that far away day had occurred, all unbeknownst to him, The Convergence of the Twain.

Of course the event served to increase his belief in the prevalence of plots of all descriptions and for the first time − or at least the first time of which I was aware − I fell under suspicion. In the immediate aftermath I suggested that if it was possible, or the lawyers thought it advisable, I should be called to testify to the uniqueness of the occasion on which the book was presented. This was decided against, but not before Paddy had expressed his suspicions to one of the lawyers. 'I don't know who I can trust any longer', he said. 'I'm not even sure if I can trust Cronin.' As it turned out, my father had worked for years for the solicitor in question. 'If he's anything like his father you can trust him with your life', he said, a reply which Paddy had the grace to tell me of immediately.

On the night it all ended he and I and his brother went to the nearby Ormond Hotel. At least four of Paddy's women friends were in and about the place, hoping to be the chosen sympathiser, but we secluded ourselves in an inner room, and there we attempted a statement. When we failed to make much fist of a joint attempt the brother suggested that we should sit down separately, make drafts and then compare and combine them. 'After all, we're all writers here', he said. To which Paddy replied with comic resignation, 'Ay, ay. All brothers of the pen'.

The lawyers countermanded the issue of a statement because an appeal had been decided on. Then the question of costs was discussed between the brothers. Fearing secrets, I attempted to leave, but was told peremptorily to stay. I learned at least a good deal about Paddy's circumstances that I had not known before, including the fact that he was not as badly off as he had led us to believe. He had at least a proprietory interest in the farm and throughout all the years in Dublin he was in receipt of money from it. Thus, although frequently without cash, he may be regarded as a man with a small private income which, of course, was utterly inadequate to his needs. In the event the question of his having to pay costs never arose. His lawyers appealed; after prolonged argument before the Supreme Court a retrial was ordered;

the ancient weekly journal which had published the article was of course utterly unable to sustain further legal action; a small settlement was accordingly arranged; and there the matter died.

Kavanagh had pinned his hopes of fortune on the libel action and had been sorely disappointed. He took some consolation from what nowadays would be called the coverage it got. For day after day there was a two page spread in the *Irish Times*. Costello, whatever else he had done, had certainly succeeded in 1954, by his cross-examination and the responses it elicited, in adding to the Kavanagh legend. People who had never read a line of poetry; who were not sufficiently in the Dublin swim to have heard the Kavanagh jokes and the Kavanagh stories; who did not frequent his pubs; were now aware that they had a poet in their midst. 'I'm as famous as De Valera', he said one day. And then he changed his mind and pitched it higher. 'No. I'm as famous as Martin Moloney,' he declared, naming the wonder jockey of the era. And though he might have intended through his answers and statements to give another picture of the poet, the one that had emerged was oddly like the stereotype the race had cherished since the days of Eoghan Ruadh: the poet was mild, indigent, gregarious, verbally fluent and over-fond of a drop. Since we were shortly to enter a time when good people in the suburbs and elsewhere who cared nothing for poetry and had no intention of troubling themselves with it were yet to feel, and to be encouraged to feel, that they should know something at least about it, even if only on a personality level, Kavanagh had a head start. When that day dawned, as it was just about to, he would be 'the poet'. Thus, in a sense, one of his ambitions was achieved. The shadowy laureateship was his.

Dead as Doornails The Dolmen Press

Thom Gunn   **My Cambridge**

I almost didn't go to Cambridge. My headmaster thought I should, and I thought I should, but my father wasn't sure. I wasn't bright enough to get a college scholarship and my father wasn't poor enough for me to apply for a state scholarship. So while I did National Service there was the possibility that I might not actually get there: it was in any case dreadfully distant, an escape from the drudgery of the army into the bright and tranquil life of the mind. I wrote a poem addressed to Cambridge. 'Shall I ever rest on your learned lawns?' I enquired. That was my image of it, a lot of serene young men sitting around on the Backs reading serious books.

So when, during a first roll-call of freshmen in Great Hall at Trinity, a student answered his name with 'Here Sergeant', and I joined the general titter, it was from relief. We were here at last in Cambridge, actually on the site of learned lawns. We had entered the tradition.

I certainly didn't perceive the snobbery involved. I would have warmly denied it indeed, because my expectation of the place was largely based on the picture given of it in E. M. Forster's *The Longest Journey*. I expected a lot of Ansells and Rickeys, and exciting talks about ideas.

And Cambridge itself collaborated with my expectations. The Master of the college, G. M. Trevelyan, who was by then a very small bent old man, had all the new boys to tea early in that first term, and told us sweetly and learnedly about the buildings and history that we were now the latest instalment of. He showed us an Elizabethan ceiling with great pendulous decorations like stalactites which had been discovered in this century above a false ceiling of a later date, put up when Tudor things had become unfashionable. And he described how one Master, Bentley, had locked all the Fellows in a room until they gave in to his requirements for palatial alterations to his Lodge.

Meanwhile for us there were bedmakers to bring up our shaving water, there were meals in the big shadowy Hall, there was the crisp beauty of the buildings — Neville's Court for perfection, Great Court for show, and Whewell's Court for living in. And even Whewell's Court, where I was for all three years, was a fine example of heavy Victorian Gothic.

One of my contemporaries arrived at Cambridge with a broad Yorkshire accent. But this was 1950, and he made it his business to reform it, so that by the end of the year he was talking through his teeth as affectedly as any of the young gents at the Pitt Club. I wonder if he has since changed it back again.

I was reading English, and shared supervisions with a wonderful Manxman called Seth Caine. We were studying *Piers Plowman* when we found that as members of Trinity all we had to do was ask the librarian and he would show us the fifteenth-century manuscripts in the Wren Library. So we went. He was kind to us and perhaps slightly amused, since we had come not so much to satisfy scholarly curiosity as to test our power.

But historic elegance, detached enlightenment and the life of the mind just about summed up my first year at Cambridge. I read Chaucer and discovered Donne. My supervisor, Helena Shire, worked me hard, and I liked her very much. I tried to smoke a pipe, but kept on coming across a residue of bitter juices from former attempts which was most unpleasant. This was in my first term, when I also toyed with the idea of buying a blazer, and wrote a series of poems about dejected old men walking through dead leaves. Then I became a pacifist. Then I read aloud from left-wing poetry of the 'thirties at meetings of CUSC, the socialist club, with John Mander, an Etonian Marxist two or three years younger than I, who was writing poetry that seems good to me even today. I couldn't help noticing that his poetry had a vigour somewhat lacking in mine. And as I got toward the end of the academic year I couldn't help feeling, also, that perhaps rather more might have happened to me than the life of the mind. It certainly did seem that there could be parties a bit more exciting than CUSC meetings: one saw dashing undergraduates hurrying *somewhere,* gowns flapping in the wind, and it was evidently toward parties one wasn't asked to. The truth was, I had the desire to be a social climber, but not the talent. I couldn't even find the bottom rung of the ladder, if there was one.

But just at the end of my first year, something did happen. I had a poem published in an anti-war issue of an undergraduate magazine, *Cambridge Today.* The poem was written after seeing the Lewis Milestone film, *A Walk in the Sun,* and was predictably Audenesque in idiom. But people reacted to it, another magazine's editor mentioned it in print, and I felt very encouraged. I tore up the poems about the old men and decided to work hard at writing poetry all summer.

The summer vacation was in fact as important as the whole of the preceding year. I read the whole of Shakespeare, and doing that, Helena Shire later remarked, adds a cubit to anybody's stature. And one day, hitch-hiking along a long narrow dusty road in France, I experienced a revelation of physical and spiritual freedom that I still refer to in my thoughts as the Revelation. It was like the elimination of some enormous but undefined problem that had been across my way and prevented me from moving forward. But now I suddenly found I had the energy for almost anything. And wherever I was, working in a farm camp, hitch-hiking through France, and later studying my books at my aunt's in Kent, I pushed myself through an apprenticeship in poetry. I was greatly influenced by Auden still — in one poem I even addressed Picasso as 'Sir', imitating Auden's Hopkinsey invocation to God, 'Sir, no man's enemy . . . ' And Donne gave me the licence both to be obscure and to find material in the contradictions of one's own emotions. But I wrote steadily, averaging about a poem a week, and was to continue doing so without stop for at least another year and a half.

Right from the start the second year was busier than the first. Apparently that single, derivative poem had had the authority to get me taken seriously by the other poets. That autumn a group of us would get together every week to discuss each other's work — Norman Buller and Harold Silver, I think, and maybe I knew John Coleman that early, and John Mander, who was still a communist but was soon to become an Anglo-Catholic and amaze me with talk of heresies, a word I had seen in print but had never heard spoken before. They were good practical little meetings, as I remember, in which we tried to suppress our own vanities and be of help to each other.

One windy autumn night I was walking along Jesus Lane from one of these meetings. Coming to the corner of Sidney Sussex Street, I could see my own window above. Friends would shout up to me from this street corner, to save themselves climbing two flights of stairs to find if I was in. I noticed that I had left my light on and found myself imagining that I had called my name aloud and could now see my own head stick out of the window above. There were times when anything seemed possible.

Meanwhile I was going to all of F. R. Leavis's lectures, though it was earlier, at the end of the previous year, that I had discovered him. He attracted me as few other teachers at Cambridge did: it is true that his lectures were prepared monologues like everybody else's, but they seemed to have the improvisatory character of discussions. And he was frank about his passion for literature — it was for him important because of its bearing upon experience, no less. If this passion sometimes made him argumentative or undignified, so much the worse for those he argued with, it all helped to validate his approach. I could see it all, this commitment to literature, as neither pastime nor occasion for scholarship, it was after all the reason I had wanted to read English in the first place. And his discriminations and enthusiasms helped teach me to write, better than any creative writing class could have. His insistence on the realized, being the life of poetry, was exactly what I needed. His perceptions about language and verse movement in discussing the first line of *Burnt Norton*, of Wordsworth's 'Surprised by joy', of 'If it were done when 'tis done', for example — by going directly to the texture of poetry, by showing how the reader's halting and attentive voice is an equivalent to the poet's act of exploration, by risking close scrutiny that entered into the terms of creation — brought me right to the hearth of my own activity. I was the victim of large, vague, diffused emotions. Seeing them as too diffused I had tried to turn my back on them, and had written my poems about old men who possessed only minimal emotions. But Leavis's lectures helped me to deal directly with my own, by reducing their diffusion, by concentrating them.

Yet there was an orthodoxy. I had to learn without becoming a disciple, for disciples have a tendency to turn observation into doctrine. But I was not after all one of Leavis's students and indeed met him only once personally, and then it was in my third year. So I learnt what I could and then ran off with it. Which is not to say that I don't look back upon his lectures with gratitude and love.

I was to have several close friends who read English at Leavis's college, Downing, but they were all in some way a bit alienated from the master himself. It was in fact about this time, at the beginning of my second year, that I met a brilliant young freshman from Downing, a Scot named Karl Miller. Argumentative, inquisitive, imaginative, he seemd to have no preconceived ideas of what he might find at Cambridge and he wasn't going to accept anybody else's. His very abrasiveness was part of his charm. And he charmed me off my feet, as he did everybody whom he didn't irritate, and I stuck by his side, all admiration, for the next year.

When I wrote a new poem I would give it to him for criticism, and he would pin it to the wall above his desk for several days before he told me what he thought of it. He helped me in other and greater ways. He matured my mind amazingly, and I learned from his habit of questioning, of questioning everything. There was always something rather childish about the way I submitted to the enthusiasms of others. If I learned to argue with them a little, it was from him.

I no longer wanted to be a social climber. The people I knew now were much too exciting for me to want to go beyond them. Another friend from Downing was John Coleman, a poet and reviewer. He was so wise and worldly that I was once heard to say, 'Five minutes with John Coleman and all my problems are solved.' His affectionately witty manner struck me as the last word in sophistication. I wrote a poem to him beginning 'You understand both Adolphe and Fabrice'. And he did too, though he was not to be without his problems. Some time after I first knew him he was walking one evening with a girl on a Cambridge street, neither of them in the black gowns students were then supposed to wear after dark. Proctors appeared to question them; they answered with assumed voices and farcical accents, for which they were sent down from Cambridge.

Meanwhile, independently of my friends, I was trying to develop certain thoughts. They amounted to a rather crude theory of what I called; 'pose', based partly on the dramatics of John Donne, somewhat perhaps on Yeat's theory of masks, and most strongly on the behaviour of Stendhal's heroes. I was to find support for it from other sources, notably from some of Shakespeare's characters, like the Bastard in *King John* and Coriolanus, and later from Sartre. It was, as you can see, literary in character, but its principal source was the Revelation on the road in France, with its intimations of unbounded energy. The theory of pose was this: everyone plays a part, whether he knows it or not, so he might as well deliberately design a part, or a series of parts, for himself. Only a psychopath or a very good actor is in danger of *becoming* his part, however, so one who is neither is left in an interesting place somewhere in between the starting point — the bare undefined and undirected self, if he ever existed — and the chosen part.

This is a place rich in tensions between the achieved and the unachieved. I thought of Julien Sorel with Madame Rénal, the counterpoint a man's vulnerable emotions made upon his seduction timed by the clock.

To tell the truth, I don't remember doing much about my theory in the actual living of my life, but viewing myself as an actor trying to play a part provided rich material for poetry. It also provided opportunities for falling flat on my face once I forgot the more ridiculous possibilities implicit in the whole theory. One of the poems I wrote during this year was called 'A Village Edmund', referring to Edmund in *King Lear*. It concluded thus:

> *'When it was over he pulled his trousers on.*
> *"Demon lovers must go," he coldly said.*
> *And she stared at the pale intolerable moon.'*

Towards the end of my second year I met Tony White, another student from Downing. I had been aware of him for a long time, as many others had, for he was a rising local actor. He had played, or shortly was to play, Aufidius, Astrov, Gaveston, Mark Antony (in *Julius Caesar*), Petruchio, Romeo, and Cyrano, among other parts, as romantic-existentialist characters. The similarity between the parts is not great, perhaps it was an error that he made it so, but the vigour of the interpretations amounted to a unifying style. If his Aufidius was slightly more sensitive than one would have expected, one might almost say more alienated, then his Romeo was also more of a tough than he is usually seen to be. For his interpretation of Romeo, indeed, Tony took as a guiding hint the scene with the apothecary near the end — a certain callousness qualifies the romantic obsession, but maybe also makes his absorption in it possible. But in all the parts, as he played them, there was a kind of athletic defiance of the gods.

We first met at a party, where we joyfully discussed Stendhal for about two hours. We were later to find many other shared enthusiasms. But, well as I came to know him at Cambridge, I think I took him at face value at this time, and it was easy to do so, his surface was so finished, so lively and delightful in itself. He was a man of courtesy, and I mean courtesy not merely in a social sense. It was a giving of himself, in all his strength and sweetness, to others, whom he admired more than he could ever admire himself. His courtesy was a direct result of the deep unease in him, a defiance of it. And ultimately he wasn't able to keep up the kind of self-regard which would have been necessary for him to continue as an actor.

Anyway, from the time I met him till his death as the result of a football accident at the age of forty-five, he was one of the most important people in my life. If I was not yet to learn the real vulnerabilities in him for a while (and they were vulnerabilities that in others would have seemed like strengths), we were still becoming tied to each other by mutual enthusiasm. He seemed to articulate in a bolder way than I ever could the kind of personal freedom that I had glimpsed on the road in France: he was a model as well as a friend. He helped me to shape my thoughts. It was he who first got me to read Sartre's plays and Camus' novels. (They were not yet taught in universities). He introduced me to his friends who had already left Cambridge. We formed projects together, we studied books together, we even found, to our amusement, that we both affected the same check shirts, which we had bought on Charing Cross Road, making us look, we hoped, more like Canadian loggers than Cambridge undergraduates.

I have a card from him which must date from a bit later, the beginning of 1954:

> All my best wishes for
> panache, logique, espagnolisme,
> l'imprévu, singularité and
> **MAGNANIMITY**
> in the New Year
> from one Étranger
> to another

He was certainly fully aware of the comic implications of our home-made philosophy, the mélange of Rostand, Stendhal, Shakespeare, and Camus.

Cambridge had not before seemed so rich in its fulfilment of possibilities. I had a lot of exciting friends, I was doing well in my exams, and there was the summer. The winter of Cambridge is so bleak, so unremitting, that the early summer always seems like a gift; it is even greater than anything one could possibly have *earned* by suffering through the other seasons. I have memories of charming idylls such as every undergraduate has always had: of sitting on the Backs in early evening listening to the long calls of the birds as they went to their nests, of bicycling out past the fields to supervisions at Conduit Head Road and once of clearing the orchard there with a billhook, and of a time very close before exams when some of us took off the afternoon and punted down to Grantchester and back, Karl Miller improvising ballads about the people in the boat, particularly about Geoffrey Strickland, in stanzas that started 'Now old Sir Geoffrey . . .'

And a play was put on, *The Taming of the Shrew.* Toby Robertson directed it, his sister Toppit played Katherine, Tony White played Petruchio, and other friends like Sasha Moorsom were in it. I was persuaded to play First Servant, and as Second Servant almost never turned up to rehearsals I got his lines too. It was played during May Week, three nights in Trinity Fellows' Garden and three nights in King's Fellows' Garden. In the last scene as night came on, the servants held up flaming torches. It was Cambridge at its sweetest — Shakespeare, the moonlit summer night, the park-like private gardens of wealthy colleges, friends I hoped would be friends for life — different kinds of happiness rolled into one.

Yet there was no fixed Cambridge. There was instead a number of beautifully kept-up old buildings and a core of teachers and retainers. This was a background against which a lot of intelligent young people improvised their fantasies of what 'Cambridge' might be. The fantasies could be sporty or scholarly, they might be about artistic community or gilded youth, but they were all essentially derivative, and it was the derivativeness that provided continuity. My Forsterian fantasy had been brought up to date but also enriched and extended by the fantasies of my friends. And apparently, whether we were conscious of it or not, our fantasies — which we speedily fulfilled — had to do with success.

I conclude this, not because I can remember making my bid for local fame, but because in my third year I got it and people seldom become successful without wanting to be. There was always a niche for the Cambridge Poet (as for the Cambridge Politician, the Cambridge Editor, and the Cambridge Actor), and I was indeed happy to occupy it now that John Mander had given up writing. I edited an anthology of student poetry. I was now president of the English Club, with Karl doing the hard work, as secretary. As such, I gave embarrassed introductions to Angus Wilson, Henry Green, Dylan Thomas (sober and punctual), W. W. Robson, Kathleen Raine, Bonamy Dobrée, William Empson, and other writers who came to speak to us. And Mark Boxer (the cartoonist Marc) asked me to help with the magazine *Granta,* of which he was editor, but that worked out only for a short time, even though I continued to publish in it.

Looking back on that time, I can see it all as a bit incestuous: we promoted each other consistently. For example, the university newspaper *Varsity* featured a profile of a local celebrity each week, and it seems to me that we all wrote each other's profiles, thus creating and perpetuating each other's celebrity.

I now went to as many chic parties as I wanted to, but I wanted to less and less. I had a sense of the whole thing stiffening, there was less of that fine feeling of flexibility that there had been the year before.

I do remember one remarkable party, or rather Karl told me about it because I passed out from drinking about a half-gallon of sherry. It took place at Newnham, and a don had to be specially brought from her bed, in her nightdress and dressing-gown, to open a side gate, normally locked, so that I could be carried more easily to a waiting taxi. She stood there in pained silence, waiting to give permission for the closing of the gate, and it seems that as I was being hauled past her my unconscious body gave a terrific fart, as if adding the sin of ingratitude to that of gluttony. I do not remember this personally, but I have Karl's word for it.

There was later a memorable escapade. About six of us, three boys and three girls, decided to go to Paris for a week. So after my yearly Christmas job with the post office, I went over to stay with John Coleman, who was now teaching in a school near there. The place he had borrowed from a gym teacher was far too small, so we all moved to a cheap hotel on the Rue Jacob, sleeping in two rooms. Paris was iron-cold, and we had a wonderful time, though I can't remember the order in which things happened very well. The group kept separating, reforming, and separating again. We ate horsemeat steaks and black sausage on the Boulevard St-Germain. Tony had met a French girl on the boat and she asked him and me round to dinner with her family, where the father kept putting down Shakespeare as a barbarian who couldn't observe the unities. We saw *Phèdre* at the Comédie Française, done in much the same style as in the seventeenth century. One of us, John Holmstrom, bought some books by Genet, which he intended to smuggle back into England, these being banned books. And I found myself somehow spending the end of New Year's Eve alone in someone else's room at the top of a smelly tenement. I opened the windows before I went to sleep and drunkenly watched the big damp snowflakes as they fell though the patch of light. A couple of days later Tony and Bronwyn O'Connor and I returned across the Channel together, sitting on the deck singing music-hall songs so that we wouldn't think about being sick.

Then we went back for our last two terms at Cambridge. The best thing about being an undergraduate at Oxford or Cambridge was that you were trusted to do the work more or less in your own time and to feed on what authors you would. I now went to almost no lectures in English, but to some in the French and History Faculties. And it must have been around this time that I realized I was getting more education from my contemporaries than from my teachers. Moreover I don't think I met any teachers at Cambridge in the whole of my first two years, apart from my supervisors. In my third year I did meet a few, but largely because I went to the right parties.

Meanwhile Mark Boxer was sent down for 'blasphemy', because *Granta* published a poem uncomplimentary to God. Its sophistication is sufficiently indicated by the lines, 'You drunken gluttonous seedy God,/You son of a bitch, you snotty old sod.' It is hard to believe that such a poem should have caused a scandal, and in fact the scandal was caused only for the Proctors. But it was the Proctors who had the power to send Mark down and to ban *Granta* for a year. However, some undergraduates, graduates, and dons revived the magazine under the name of *Gadfly,* of which the format and contributors were identical. It even contained drawings by Mark.

One morning I read in the *News Chronicle* of Dylan Thomas's death. Karl had taught me to love his poetry. I went round to Karl's room and, not finding him there, left a solemn little note on his mantelpiece: 'This is a black day for English poetry', so that he should know I was feeling the proper grief.

And from around this time I find an issue of a mimeographed periodical called *Broadsheet,* in which a reviewer ends his piece with these words: 'Since writing this article I have met E. J. Hughes, of

Pembroke, who is trying to bring writers of poetry in Cambridge together at the Anchor, where the landlord has set aside a room for the display of poetry.' E. J. Hughes of Pembroke was very retiring. I am not sure if I even knew him to speak to while I was at Cambridge, though I did know what he looked like. We did not become friends until years later, after he had, as Ted Hughes, published his first book.

As the year went on, I withdrew more and more from the 'Cambridge' I had helped create. I had fallen in love, but that is another story. In any case I felt a pull away from the place.

In the summer I hung on after the term was over, deciding for indefinite reasons to take my degree in person, in wing collar, bow tie, and rented suit. Most of my friends did it by proxy and it was already tourist season, the Backs and the river covered by straying families with cameras and sandwiches. But I was still a part of it for a few more days before I joined the families as one who had no place here.

What I was to realize more clearly after I had gone down was that, for all who go there, whether rich or poor (or, most likely, middle-class), Cambridge is a place of privilege, and things are usually made easier for those who have been there. My first books were reviewed more kindly than they deserved largely, I think, because London expected good poets to emerge from Oxford and Cambridge and here I was, somebody new with all the fashionable influences and coming from Cambridge. I am not implying that those who treated me so well when I started publishing were consciously playing favourites, but I know that they were mostly from Oxford and Cambridge themselves and that *I got a hearing* more readily than if I had just graduated from the University of Hull.

Many of my contemporaries went on to become well known − as directors of plays, actors, editors of magazines, historians, reviewers, novelists, dramatists. London received them warmly, and being talented they flourished in the warmth. Only Tony White, among my close friends, became an exception: he joined the Old Vic company, and had got so far after a few years as to play Cassio in *Othello* when he dropped it all, for a life of odd jobs and translating, barely making ends meet as a handy man, plumber, house painter, or translator of some lengthy anthropological work from French into English. He dropped out, coolly and deliberately, from the life of applause, having come to see how the need for it complicates one's existence quite unnecessarily.

So I am grateful to Cambridge for many things. It enriched my life enormously, it gave me the security and advantages that everybody ought to have, but it also brought me up against someone who could eventually teach me that the real business was elsewhere completely.

My Cambridge , Robson Books